This book is bound to guide those just starting their career, already working and the retired to prepare early for the benefits of a comfortable life in retirement.

PREPARING FOR A HAPPY AND COMFORTABLE LIFE IN RETIREMENT

A GUIDE TO A COMFORTABLE LIFE IN RETIREMENT

ZACHARIAH DAUKE SULEIMAN MNIM

Copyright @2020 by Zachariah Suleiman

All rights reserved. No part of this book may be reproduced in any form or by any electronic or mechanical means, including information storage and retrieval systems, without permission in writing from the publisher, except by reviewers, who may quote brief passages in a review.

This publication contains the opinions and ideas of its author. It is intended to provide helpful and informative material on the subjects addressed in the publication. The author and publisher specifically disclaim all responsibility for any liability, loss or risk, personal or otherwise, which is incurred as a consequence, directly or indirectly, of the use and application of any of the contents of this book.

WORKBOOK PRESS LLC
187 E Warm Springs Rd,
Suite B285, Las Vegas, NV 89119, USA

Website: https://workbookpress.com/
Hotline: 1-888-818-4856
Email: admin@workbookpress.com

Ordering Information:
Quantity sales. Special discounts are available on quantity purchases by corporations, associations, and others.
For details, contact the publisher at the address above.

ISBN-13:   978-1-953839-65-7 (Paperback Version)
            978-1-953839-66-4 (Digital Version)

REV. DATE: 18/11/2020

Dedicated to all workers who've just started work, are already working, and the retired

Preface

The first edition of this book was written out of my knowledge and experience with the wider society on how investment could be used to change the lives of individuals who properly utilize their hard-earned funds on assets that have positive cash flows. It was my first. I was motivated and excited at the potential I had already found in the experiences of those who had utilized the principles in my first book to succeed.

The responses I received from my first book encouraged me to have a review of the book, which led to this new edition you are reading today. While reviewing the book, I realized that the greater part of the book concentrated on the need to utilize one's hard-earned income on assets that could bring in money into one's system without looking at the need to prepare early for retirement. I also discovered that a lot of people neither saw the need to prepare early for retirement nor identify those areas of interest they intended to go into early enough before thinking of retirement. Consequently, the need to encourage people to prepare early became imperative. The prerequisites required for looking ahead for a happy and comfortable life in retirement includes early preparation, making the right choices, and taking positive actions on the issues of life. The issues of life that have a significant effect on everyone are the focus of this book.

The need to prepare early for retirement then became obvious when I met some of my seniors and retired colleagues who, incidentally, did not find it expedient to prepare early for their retirement. They waited until they were retired before thinking of what to do with their lives. Their mistakes and subsequent experience also contributed to encouraging me write this book to draw the attention of those of us about to start work, still working, or retired to have a rethink on the issues of life that deserve our greater attention and absolute portion of our mindset. Early preparation is a necessity if we intend to have a happy and comfortable life in retirement. The basic foundations of our existence revolve around the factors that affect our choices and the actions we take in life.

In this book, I intend to share the experience of those who have retired and the issues of life as they affect retirement life. The focus of this book is on three groups of people. The first group are those who have just started their working career or are about to, the second group are those already working or about to retire, and the third group are those already in retirement. Whichever group you belong to, the focus of this book is beneficial to you and the people around you. Whether you have just started work today or already working for some years or retired, you need to address certain issues of your life, reset your mindset, and make choices and take steps that will ensure you end this life positively.

In researching for this book, I discovered how effectively the resilient drive and the ability of people who had limited resources to start life with made them pursue their purpose with passion and imbibed change, and they ended up being happy and successful in the society. That habit of resilience in the pursuit of their purpose with passion, imbibing change, influenced them and the lives of several other people around them. The several questions I received from many people who read my first book, the expressions of regret from those who had retired without preparing early, and the expressions of concern from those working on how to prepare for retirement made me set up the ambitious task of reaching more people to share in the knowledge I have acquired through personal efforts and interest.

I also had the privilege of talking to hundreds of workers and retired people in and out of employment. From the discussions I had, it brought to light the different shades of opinion people have on the topic of retirement. Many people I talked to did not want to think of preparing for retirement as they felt thinking of it amounted to wishing them early exit from the luxury of steady income, comfortable official cars, and residence and travel incentives. What they failed to realize is that whether they think about it or not and prepare or not, one day they will retire.

I will, therefore, present in the first chapter of this book the necessity of preparing early for retirement, and in the second chapter, efforts are made to appeal to those who are just starting their career to brace for the reality of the need to prepare early for retirement. The attention of those already working is drawn for them to make the necessary efforts to prepare and identify what they intend to do when their working days are over. Those already retired are not left out as efforts are also made to share the experience of others with them. Outside this, the issues of life are discussed on the subsequent chapters to let all appreciate those issues that could affect life generally and retirement life in particular. The impact of the comfort zone is also presented in the last chapter.

It is my hope that as you read this book, from the need to prepare early for retirement, the experience of the past from those who have retired ahead of us and the issues of life that are identified, presented, and analyzed will be your real guide for a happy and comfortable life in retirement.

Zachariah Dauke Suleiman
Lagos, Nigeria

ACKNOWLEDGEMENTS

The act of writing a book is a collective effort and, therefore, has to be acknowledged. Consequently, I am most grateful to Almighty God, who bestowed on me the inspiration to write when, humanly speaking, I thought I could not.

In preparing for this book, I talked to many retired people about their experience in retirement and asked what sort of information they would want passed to others about to start work or working and about to retire. I also enquired on what information they wished they had been given in the past. Many of them were generous with their advice, and I have passed it on with thanks to them.

I must acknowledge the input of Dr Chris Yere, faculty of business administration; Professor Ishaya Haruna Nock, Ahmadu Bello University, Zaria; Professor Amos Yabaya, dean, faculty of microbiology, Kaduna State University, Kaduna, Nigeria; Mr Musa Aduwak, former deputy press secretary to the federal government of Nigeria; and Mr Sanni Musa Babatunde, general manager, corporate audit, Nigerian National Petroleum Corporation (NNPC) for their relentless effort in reading the manuscript and critiquing the book.

I also want to acknowledge my mentor, Dr Joseph Maiyaki, former director general, Centre for Management Development, Lagos, Nigeria, who inspired and encouraged me. He painstakingly proofread the book.

I sincerely thank my employers, the NNPC, where my working life and the need to prepare early for retirement evolved. I thank the management and staff for giving me the opportunity to grow and improve myself to the level of writing this book.

To my colleagues at the Brass LNG and others too numerous to mention, I sincerely thank them for the useful discussion through which I experimented and tested the acceptability of the ideas of this book.

To the management of Kazlight Global Nigeria Limited, especially the managing director, Mr Iliya Usman, who assisted in formatting the book, I thank you for the support and encouragement.

I also appreciate my wife, Mrs Martina Zachariah, Esq. for bringing in her legal professional eye while reading the manuscript and my children for their understanding during the writing of this book.

To all the individual authors whose ideas have formed part of this book that could not be recognized, I thank them all for making their ideas available to me.

Contents

Introduction

Chapter 1

    Preparing for Retirement---14

Chapter 2

    Just Started Work--24
    The Most Crucial Phase of Your Life------------------------------------25
    Start Early in Life---26
    Take Positive Steps---27
    The Three Pillars of Life---29
    Acquire the Necessary Skills--30
    Apply the Knowledge Acquired---32
    Focus on the Things That Make You Happy------------------------33
    Your Source of Income Will Not Last Forever--------------------34

Chapter 3

    The Working Class--36
    Prepare Emotionally---37
    Prepare Psychologically---39
    Prepare Financially---40
    Centre Your Retirement on Your Passion-------------------------------43

Chapter 4

    The Retired--47
    Surplus Time---48

Leaving Behind a Comfortable Life --------------------------------- 50
Adjustment Time --- 51
The Better Phase of Life --- 52
Periodically Review Your Retirement ------------------------------ 53
Develop a Positive Mindset

Chapter 5

Money Matters --- 56
Different Ways of Acquiring Money -------------------------------- 61
Fundamental Ways of Handling Money ------------------------------- 67

Chapter 6

Investment Matters --- 78
Other Aspects of Investment -------------------------------------- 81
Types of Investments --- 90
Investing in the Banking Sector ---------------------------------- 93
Investing in the Capital Market ---------------------------------- 94
Investing in Real Estate
Investing in Your Own Business ----------------------------------- 99
Managing Investment --- 100

Chapter 7

Success Matters --- 106
Phases of Success --- 111
Roadblocks to Success --- 112
Managing Success -- 125

Chapter 8

Setback Matters --- 131
Why Do People Fail? --- 136

Managing Setbacks --- 144

Chapter 9

The Comfort Zone -- 149
Effect of the Comfort Zone -- 156
Way out of the Comfort Zone --- 160

Conclusion -- 165

About the Author --- 167

References -- 169

Chapter 1
PREPARING FOR RETIREMENT

A surprising number of people work long hours up to the day they retire and, on the first day of their retirement, are completely unprepared for the prospect of having nothing specific to do for the rest of their lives. Many of these people go through a significant trauma in the transition to retirement.

—Nic Peeling

We all came into this world the same—naked, scared, and ignorant. However, the manner or way we will end life will basically depend on our choices, which are also influenced by other factors such as the experiences of growing up, the books we read, the associations we make, and of course, our work or living environments. We have to prepare early and make choices at every stage of our lives to enhance the situation we face. We also have to take proactive actions going forward with the conditions that we will be facing after our working days are over and during our retirement.

Any time the word retirement is mentioned, different people have various impressions regarding the meaning and definition of retirement. It is also the appropriate opportunity to discuss the right time to prepare for retirement. To manage retirement is another tricky issue, as it has to do with people's emotions. For anyone to think of exiting a job he or she has been used to for some time and with the steady pay cheque, it leads to a lot of emotions as the individual considers the long-time commitments to the job and usual routine of engagement.

What then is retirement? Retirement is defined by the Oxford Dictionary as 'the act of stopping a particular type of work especially sports, politics, etc.' To retire is to stop someone from a job in which he receives paid compensation. To retire from one's job is to stop doing your job especially because you have reached a particular age or a stipulated time of service. Retirement, therefore, is the act of leaving a job either because you have reached or completed a stipulated time of service or voluntarily decided to disengage from your service. It could be as a result of compulsory requirement by an organization that demands the stoppage of your work.

In most countries, there are mandatory times and ages expected of public and private workers to work and retire. The particular age for retirement differs from country to country and for different jobs in both public and private organizations. In Nigeria, for instance, various chronological ages at which one retires are seventy for judges; university academics used to retire at sixty but now seventy; state civil servants at fifty-five; federal civil servants, sixty; and many organizations in the private sector, sixty and sixty-five, depending on the company. However, workers in the public sector are expected to retire from service after thirty-five years or when such individual reaches the ages of sixty, whichever comes first. The United States of America (USA), for instance, through its Social Security Act (1935), designated the people age sixty-five and above as aged. While the official retirement age in the USA is sixty-five years old, irrespective of which sector of the economy (public or private) one works.

When it comes to the issue of retirement, there are many exit points in the life of a worker. The exit point includes resigning from the job voluntarily or your employer could decide to terminate or even dismiss you when you disobey or engage in illegal activities that are contrary to the laid-down rules and regulations of the organization. Downsizing could edge you out of a job. Sickness and incapacitation could lead to sudden retirement, which has its challenges. That job or employment and all the luxuries associated to the steady pay cheque being enjoyed will, one day, come to an end. Sickness or health issues could affect your performance and employment, which could lead to the end of your working life. Whether you think about it or prepare early for retirement or not, you will leave that job one day. Even if you are healthy, obedient, efficient, and effective, the issue of old age could see you out of that job.

What became clearer, as I talked to hundreds of workers, was the fact that you have the choice of preparing early for retirement or resign to faith and wait for the time your working life is over. You have to choose whether to act now or not. What you choose to plan for and take action for today will affect your future. It is worthwhile to take action today regarding your job and retirement. You have to be proactive and start preparing for the end from the beginning. Whatever you envisage or think of engaging in after retirement in the future will depend on the actions you choose to take today. The comfort—or otherwise—of your retirement will be a product of your actions today. The way you prepare your bed, so shall you lay on it. If you prepare your bed well, the sleep on it will definitely be smooth and sweet.

My experience at the beginning of my work career lacked emphasis on the need to look ahead into the future and prepare early for the realities of retirement. The realities of retirement were viewed as too far in the future that they did not desire early preparation. However, I have come to realize through research and interaction that the realities of the future have to be prepared for now if one desires to have a happy and comfortable retirement life. To have a happy and comfortable retirement life, one must make the right choices and prepare early for it. Preparing early for retirement calls for courage, determination, and a resilient mindset that would make one to focus on the things of the future. Notwithstanding the type of retirement plan before you, it is required that you personally look outside the norm. When you look outside the norm, those things that are new and attract difficulties often become strange. You may have to put in extra effort to acquire the necessary knowledge that would enable you to appreciate the act of early preparation for retirement. Thinking outside the box could be difficult due to the effect of the comfort zone. This concept is discussed in detail in a subsequent chapter.

While there is no clear cut way or method of preparing for retirement, the basic target is to have something to fall back on in old age or at that period of retirement when you would no longer have the strength to work. This old age income would enable you to confront some of the challenges (health costs) as well as costs of leisure, family, societal responsibilities, and household bills. As you work and have the energy to continue your daily job, create wealth that would take care of your old age. While working, work towards creating wealth. Think of wealth as a tree. It takes time for it to grow, and you need to nurture and care for it as it grows.

Don't wait until you have retired to think about and prepare for your post retirement projects. When you make the right choices and prepare early for retirement, the stress of sudden change from a working life to a retirement life would be taken away from you. Those who took the time to decide early to arrange for their exit from service would usually enjoy their transition as the psychological effect would have been taken care of.

The psychological impact of changing the routine of life can be a herculean task and devastating when faced without adequate preparation. That is why Nic Peeling, in his book Brilliant Retirement, stated, 'A surprising number of people work long hours up to the day they retire and, on the first day of their retirement, are completely unprepared for the prospect of having nothing specific to do for the rest of their lives. Many of these people go through a significant trauma in the transition to retirement.' When you plan, it is said that you have prepared to succeed. When you prepare to succeed, success will come your way, and the comfort of a happy and successful/comfortable retirement will be enjoyed. When you don't plan early for your retirement, you end up discovering late that you are going through a significant trauma in the transition to retirement, completely unprepared for the prospect of having nothing to do for the rest of your life. To enjoy a happy and comfortable retirement requires a lot of planning, sacrifice, determination, and commitment to take charge of the emotional control of the resources one received during active service.

As you work and have the energy to continue your day's job, create wealth that will take care of your old age. It takes time for it to grow, and you need patience to nurture and care for it as it grows. That also calls for adjustments and subtle changes in the utilization of the income that you work for. You need to take the time to discipline your habit by making the right choices and plans that would ensure that your income is invested in ventures that would ensure that your income yields you wealth at your retirement.

The issue of the amount being paid and the need to set something aside from this amount can be challenging. We are aware of what some workers are being paid, which could be less than what they require for their upkeep, not to talk of what they will save for preparing early for retirement. The thought of the amount being paid and the need to set something aside from that meagre amount can appear to be a genuine reason not to save.

Consequently, we are often tempted to make all sorts of excuses, which may becloud our ability to commit to preparing for retirement early. This is the case of a worker who made this statement: 'How do you plan adequately for retirement without good wages? How do you save money for retirement when what you earn is not enough to cater to your immediate need? You have to survive first before you can think and plan for the future.' This statement was genuinely made by someone who felt the realities of life concerning the amount he received as salary, which was not sufficient for him, and to think of setting aside a part of it was almost impossible. However, the truth is, it is not the quantum of what you receive as salary that matters but the self-discipline, self-mastery, and self-control you have to manage even the little you receive. If you do not discipline yourself with the little you receive, even if you receive a huge amount of money, it would be difficult to save and invest.

If you are an employee, it is not what you do from 8 a.m.–5 p.m. that counts. It is what you do with your pay cheque / salary after you receive it that actually counts. In other words, what you do from 8 a.m.–5 p.m. is your profession or your job. What you do with your pay cheque / salary is your business. It isn't how much money you make that counts; it is how much you keep and invest in assets with positive cash flow that counts. The struggle in life has to do with the mindset and the belief system that one has before him.

Financial struggle is often a direct result of people working all their lives for someone else and at the end of their working life they have nothing left for themselves due to their beliefs and mindset. The type of mindset and belief system you have will affect the manner you handle your pay cheque or salary. Those who belief their retirement is too far will definitely consider setting aside a part of their pay cheque or salary a waste. While those who believe there is the need to plan and prepare early for retirement will find no difficulty in the commitment of preparation for the future.

For you to have a happy and comfortable retirement, develop early the mindset and habit of saving part of your salary for yourself and your children. The opportunities and prosperity that come with this are better imagined. That is why it is always said that the opportunities that God sent will not wake those who are asleep. These opportunities will only meet those that are active and ready to utilize such opportunities.

Whenever you put aside an amount of money for your future or your children, you are actually paying yourselves. Any amount you retain from your salary is the only amount you actually get as you eventually give everything else away to others for their services to you. So preferably, develop the habit of paying God first and yourself second before you begin meeting your needs and everyone else's. The truth is, it is not easy to save when the amount you receive is small; however, when you develop the saving habit and start with a small amount, gradually you will get used to it, and eventually, it will increase with time. Do not start saving a large amount immediately. The problem is not in how much or how little you earn but how much or how little you spend.

Keep your daytime job, but start early saving and buying assets that have positive cash flow, not liabilities or personal effects that have no real value once you get the opportunity. Continue to convert your hard-earned income into assets and grow them. Try paying yourself no less than 10–30 per cent of your normal income and 80–90 per cent of your extra income. What determines your wealth is not how much you receive but, rather, how much you save. The paradox of money is that people tend to spend more than they earn. That is why we must learn by practising saving even when we are earning small.

Once money goes into your system, never let it come out to purchase liabilities. Think of this money as your employees. Money in your system should be money that should work hard for you as you have already worked hard to get it in. You have to always search for ways to put your money into work by converting it into assets that generate more money. You have to realize that once you receive your pay cheque or salary, you have the freedom of choice on how you are going to spend it.

Your emotions have a great role in your choices. Those who control their emotions can take time to control their ability to spend their money wisely. Those who spend their money wisely will always be more prosperous than those who have no control over their emotions. No wonder Warren Buffet, America's one-time richest investor, says, 'A person who cannot manage his or her emotions, cannot manage money'. In the real world, emotional intelligence is more important than mental intelligence if you want to become financially happy and comfortable at your retirement. If you are out of control emotionally, your chances of solving your financial challenges are reduced. If you want to improve your financial intelligence, you have to work hard on improving your emotional intelligence. As your control over your emotional intelligence improves, you will discover your investment skills also improve.

Incidentally too, a lot of people work actively during their earlier years without preparing for retirement and, consequently, do not have much to fall back on in old age or upon retirement, when they are no longer active, because they did not prepare for this period of their lives. Moreover, many people are living longer into their retirement due to modern medical facilities with fewer people available to support them during this period. Hence, many of these people end up in old people's homes at retirement or die on the queue while waiting for retirement verification. Do not let this happen to you. You, therefore, need to prepare early for your retirement to avert the experience of these people.

The usual set-up where your place of work takes care of you till death no longer holds. Things have changed. In the past, organizations also took care of their employees' retirement by guaranteeing the employees' pay cheques for as long as he/she live. As you probably already know, that is not the case today. Pension plans that pay an employee for life, called defined benefit, no longer exist. Today, very few companies offer these plans. They are simply too expensive for organizations to sustain. Today a new type of pension plan has emerged, the defined contribution plan. Such plans are known as the 401k, IRAs, Keoghs, and Nigerian Pension Plan, etc. Simply put, a defined contribution plan has no guarantee of pay cheque for life. You only get what you and your employer contribute—if you and your employer contributed—which are paid for a specific period, only not throughout life.

Companies are no longer responsible for your old age or retirement and, consequently, cannot guarantee your pay cheque when your working days are over. You have to prepare and take care of your old age and retirement after your working days are over. If you want a happy and comfortable retirement and a better old age, you have to prepare early for that aspect of your life. Retirement life will be a nightmare for those who refuse to prepare early for it or learn the basic principle of money. For many people, who will create time to learn about money while working, their retirement will be a great experience. You just can't be weak or uneducated when it comes to the game of money and investment or businesses if you want a fulfilled retirement life.

When you are preparing for your retirement, there is a need to invest in different types of investments even if you already have your retirement plan. These investments include businesses, real estates, stocks, mutual funds, and commodities. To prepare early for retirement, you need to continue to prepare, study, educate, train, and search for investments whether you have money or not. In the past, corporations and businesses provided health care and retirement benefits to their employees after their working days were over but no longer do so. Today, millions of workers earn less, while at the same time, they need more money to cover their own medical expenses and save enough for their retirement.

Saving for retirement is just getting a whole lot harder. Not only is it difficult to save as much money as you will need but also the value of the money you do save may be worth less and less as you get older. No wonder the greatest fear among most of the working class today is running out of money during retirement.

They say change is the only thing that is constant. As you work, take a look at the changes going on around you. Make efforts to understand the changes, and accept the realities of the changes occurring in your environment. The present pension scheme is different from the pension scheme of the past. There is a fundamental difference between the industrial age pension plan and the information age retirement plan. In the industrial age, companies would employ people for life and give them pension once their working days were over.

Today, companies are not giving out pension plans the way they used to. The rules have changed, and incidentally, people are retiring earlier and living longer lives. This means retirees need more financial security to take care of their long lives after retirement. They also need more sophisticated ways of building assets than were offered by the pension of the industrial age. This was well stated by Robert Kiyosaki in his book, Before You Quit Your Job: 'Today, retirees need more financial resources at retirement and more sophisticated ways of building assets than were offered by the pension plans of the Industrial Age.' The times are rapidly changing, and if you want to have a comfortable life during retirement, your approach to work, money, and investing has to change too.

If you think your financial security is the responsibility of your company or the government because of the pension plans they have, you are going to be sorely disappointed in the coming years. There is need for you to rethink on the changes taking place around you. The changes from the industrial age to the information age are the changes that are having a fundamental impact on the lives of workers all over the world. There is need to prepare for the disappointment that is coming. When you prepare for a disappointment, you would turn disappointment into an appointment. Preparing for disappointment doesn't mean you will not still be upset and concerned. But if you are prepared, it will not come as a surprise and you won't beat yourself too hard, as being too hard on yourself will make you overly cautious about taking risks or trying new ideas. When you control your emotions and use your disappointments to learn from the mistakes therein, you will discover the secrets of life.

The truth is most of us have grown up to believe that money is the root of all evil and do not see money as a good thing. Most probably, you have also been taught to work hard for money rather than have your money work hard for you and not to worry about financial future because some company or the government will take care of you when your working days are over. These beliefs would have worked for our forefathers in the industrial age but are no longer workable in the information age. What was good for our mothers and fathers is not applicable to us today. They had the opportunity of a defined benefit pension plan where they could be paid pension until death.

Today, you are expected to embark on a defined contribution pension plan where your pension will no longer be paid to you continuously until you die. Rather, you are expected to contribute, and when your working days are over, part of what you and the company have contributed will be made available for you regardless of how long you live. The rules have changed, and it is time you take control of your financial future, as the companies and government will not.

When you prepare early, therefore, you will have control of your money and retirement. Do not trust the companies and government who are expecting you to contribute a certain amount into your pension, which is handed over to those who may not have your interest in mind—the pension administrators, pension custodians, and pension managers. These people are after their individual interests, and incidentally, corruption is eating deep into their operations so that at the end of your working days, you may not get your pension money, as this money would have been affected by factors beyond the control of your pension managers. These factors could be a drastic downwards trend in the capital markets or general world depression.

In the next chapter, I will discuss from when one is just starting work to utilizing the wealth of experience gathered during the course of working life with strength and energy to getting exhausted as a result of old age and ending in retirement. The issues of transiting from active working life to retirement will also be discussed, as these can be challenging. Consequently, there will be a need to critically handle these issues in such a way that would make them beneficial to you.

Chapter 2
JUST STARTED WORK

If you wish to be successful, study success. If you wish to be happy, study happiness. If you want to make money, study the acquisition of wealth. Those who achieve these things don't do it by accident. It's a matter of studying first and practicing later.

—Jim Rohn

When growing up as a child, I had a lot of dreams and was full of expectations with regard to what the society would do for me. I was full of hopes and aspirations. When I completed school, it became clear that one would need a job to be successful in life. Starting work was an experience I was eagerly expecting, and eventually, I started work with the idea that one was young and had a lot of time ahead. Reflecting back to my early work experience, I discovered that getting a job does not guarantee success. Starting a career required a lot of counselling on issues of life relating to money, investment, and success setbacks and the effect of the comfort zone. It is my intention to share with you some of the issues of life that some of us lacked while starting our working career. Many people like me did not have the advantage of prior knowledge on these issues of life while starting down the ladder. There is a need to have some discussions with those of you just starting work in order to share those issues of life that I did not have the opportunity to get

The need to share my ideas with you came as a result of my experience when I was starting mine many years ago. I did not have the privilege of having someone speak to me on the need to think on these issues of life and the importance of preparing early for retirement. The anxiety of starting work in a lifetime can be overwhelming and interesting. It is an experience that kick-starts at the beginning of a phase in the life of the worker. Once you are able to get these issues of life right when you are starting this job, then you are on the right path. If you get them wrong, the tendency and probability is high that it may be late to realize the mistake and take a corrective measure.

The Most Crucial Phase of Your Life

If you have just started work, I want you to realize that this phase is the most crucial in your life. The way you handle this phase of your life would determine how you will end your career. This first phase of your life is important; a lot of your activities and actions will be dictated and influenced by many factors. The culture, procedures, and people existing in your organization will affect this phase of your life.

At this stage of life, a lot of people usually think that it is too early to start thinking and preparing for retirement, only to realize later that it is too late to prepare for it. However, you must bear in mind that whatever has a beginning has an end. You have to start this job with the thought of the end from the beginning. Doing this would set you apart and position you in planning and preparing early for your retirement. This was what most of those ahead of you did not do.

As you start this job, what are your goals for the future? It is not starting that job that matters; it is how you will end that career that really matters. How do you intend to end that career? What do you want to become in the future? What is your mindset on life and realities? In the next ten or twenty or even thirty years, what do you intend to be in your workplace and the society? Which part of the world do you intend to visit? What type of life do you intend to have after working and serving the organization you are just beginning to serve? What are your dreams after this active productive life? Some of us did not consider these questions when we started work, and consequently, we are still drifting and thinking of the way life will be after many years of active service. Working without a plan for retirement will affect you just as it has affected those of us who are already on our way out. Do not allow this to happen to you.

The practical steps you need to progress in life and, indeed, your workplace must, at all times, be devoid of elements of laziness and complacency. Due to youthfulness and lack of experience, the tendency of a new employee who may be influenced by bad company at the point of entry could be laziness and complacency in the life of a fresh worker. You need to be sensitive to the work environment to avoid laziness that could affect your work career. Your progress in your career and, eventually, your retirement will be dependent on your commitment to your responsibilities and value you add to your organization.

The humble will always receive the favour of all that are around him or her. When you are humble, you will be uplifted by your humility. The need for humility has to be emphasized as your progress in the workplace will depend on the manner you relate to your superiors, colleagues, and subordinates. This aspect of your life will clear the way for you to excel both within and outside the organization. You must humble yourself for you to be respected by all and sundry. What humility will bring to you after many years of efforts, arrogance will destroy within seconds. Consequently, you have to avoid arrogance if you will succeed in your career, and eventually, you will have a happy and comfortable life in retirement.

Start Early in Life

Most often, some young people like associating with the wrong company, leading them to wrong choices in life. Some make the mistake of thinking; they cannot make wealth while pursuing their passion. However, the truth is starting early in life to focus on whatever you do is what gives you an edge over others. Preparing early for retirement is one of the tasks that many people below thirty find difficult, considering the fact that life is just starting. Do not let this happen to you.

Your early days and upbringing would have been influenced by the decisions of your parents, teachers while in school, and friends before you started this job. Thisaffects the way you function and relate with your colleagues. Your mindset at the beginning of this phase will affect the end of this journey. The awareness of this mindset will propel you to start preparing early for your retirement or be complacent. Your choices in this phase of your life will affect the remaining phase.

There is, therefore, a need to prepare early in life for the life of a happy and comfortable retirement. Do not think you are too young to start preparing for your retirement life. You have to decide early on the type of life you would like to have during retirement. Identify the area of interest and passion that excites you that you intend to follow during retirement. The earlier you start identifying your passion during retirement, the better for you. Before you retire or quit that job, take time to learn all the skills that are required in the area you have chosen to spend your life on after retirement. Make efforts to understand the needed survival skills in your chosen area of interest. If you intend to be a consultant during retirement as some do, make efforts to learn the skills of consultancy while you are still working. Do not wait until you are retired before you start searching and investigating the needed requirement of being a consultant. If you have chosen to go into business, acquire the necessary skills of starting a business while working before you retire. Just as Jim Rohn would say, 'If you wish to be successful, study success. If you wish to be happy, study happiness. If you want to make money, study the acquisition of wealth. Those who achieve these things don't do it by accident. It's a matter of studying first and practicing later.'

Take Positive Steps

Your retirement life after active work or service that is still in the future can be effectively prepared for by taking positive steps today on issues of life to alter positively the life you want during retirement. If you want a positive and productive result, you need to embark on positive actions on the issues of life to enable you to achieve a different positive result. What is ahead of you and your ability to reach your goals depends on your zeal and determination to change, control, and expand your realities to achieve a happy, comfortable, and great outcome in life.

As you start this job, remember you cannot succeed in this journey alone. You have to seek first the kingdom of God and its righteousness and all these things will be added to you (Mathew 6:33). You need the direction and guidance of the Almighty God in all your activities if you want to succeed at the end of your career. In taking your decisions, you need to listen to that still little voice to guide and lead you as you struggle in life. That is why you need to trust in the Lord with all your heart and lean not on your understanding but in all your ways acknowledge Him, and He will direct your path and crown your efforts with success (Proverbs 3:5–6).

When I started work many years ago, I did not personally plan for my future until almost fifteen years after, when the idea of preparing for the future occurred to me. I know many of my colleagues were also affected, not because they knew and deliberately did not plan but because some did not have the privilege of having advisers on the subject matter or the knowledge to prepare early. Some had the knowledge but thought it was still too early to plan for their retirement.

Others have spent more than thirty years working and are about to retire without preparing early for retirement or keeping aside some amount for the future. I do not want this to happen to you. You need to be aware and focus on the future and have a new mind-set. Change, control, and expand your realities on your future and work towards achieving your set goals early in your career life when you are still strong, fresh, and full of energy. The opportunity to set your goals early in life and prepare than many of us, your elders did, is available to you; utilize it while you are still strong and energetic, and the benefits will be better imagined. What you think is real becomes your reality.

The mistake most young people make is thinking that they are still young and have more time to play around. Consequently, they tend to work for money instead of building their dreams. They often engage in a spending spree instead of careful investment ventures. They tend to procrastinate, make excuses, and apportion blames to everyone else instead of looking inwards to learn from their mistake. They like engaging in unhealthy competition with their peers instead of planning for the future. They enjoy thinking they do not need to learn further because they have learnt enough. A lot of them overburden themselves with family financial responsibilities instead of concentrating on personal development that would improve financial literacy. Some of them also like spending everything they earn and neglecting to set some money aside.

The choices you make in life will definitely determine your progress and, eventually, the level you will reach as you climb that ladder in the organization. Where you are today is a product of the choices you made in the past. The life you will face in the future will be dependent on the type of choices you will make going forward. In making your choices, efforts must be made to make sure that bad choices are kept away. To keep the bad choices away demands that you check the choices made and identify the bad ones or those that did not work; from experience, avoid repeating them whenever they seem to reappear on your path to success.

The Three Pillars of Life

The truth and realities of life lies on three pillars. These pillars are the past, the present, and the future. The past cannot be changed, but you have the ability to change the future by correcting the mistakes of the past today. If you want the future to be better than the past, you have to change, control, and expand your present reality. Your positive actions today will bring to you a desired positive future, and negative actions will equally bring a negative future. You have to effectively manage the present. Selectively forget the negative past, and create the future that you envisage.

The past, the present, and the future are the signposts of life for those who desire and intend to succeed in life. How you handle your present and future will determine the way you progress in life. The past is gone, and you may not change the choices you have made in the past. However, going forward, you can change the choices you will make. You can alter your present to change your future. The future in the life of a new worker is usually filled with great expectations, most especially when he/she is coming into the working environment for the first time. This expectation is often disrupted along the way whenever fear appears as a result of setbacks and challenges that exist in the workplace and the society.

A lot of people concentrate more on one aspect of their lives to the detriment of the other. When you concentrate more on your negative past and negative present, you will drag your future and yourself back in every moment of your life. Do not, therefore, dwell too much on your negative past. Sail away from your past and take positive actions today; otherwise, the past will continue to haunt you, as Mark Twain specifically stated, 'Twenty years from now you will be disappointed by the things that you didn't do than the things that you did do. So throw off the bowlines. Sail away from the safe harbour; catch the trade winds in your sails. Explore, Dream, Discover.'

To face the future, you must choose your dream and create your vision of the future. This vision has to be clear and straightforward. The vision constitutes what your dream looks like in your mind. For you to succeed in the future, you must be ready to pay the price of success. Have courage to take all the calculated risks that would enable you to accomplish your vision. If not, you may not accomplish your dreams. This was rightly said by Mohammed Ali: 'He who is not courageous enough to take risks will accomplish nothing in life.'

When it comes to the issue of the future, how do you treat or react to the future? What is the picture of the future before you? Do you have a target or vision or dream in life? Do you look into the future with determination to succeed, or is the future so vague that you think it may not be possible to succeed or achieve your aspirations? For you to determine the future properly, you have to look at the past and present. Where you are today is a consequence of the choices you made in the past, and where you will be in the future will definitely depend on the choices you make today.

Acquire the Necessary Skills

Looking into the future is not the only thing that will get you to the promised land; you need to acquire the necessary education and skill sets that would enable you to achieve that vision and dream. Acquiring knowledge includes reading books, attending seminars and classes, online research and study, talking with experts, and working with coaches and mentors. This information you gathered will enable you to take action. You have to look into the future and project your expectation.

In the same vein, if you want your retirement life to be happy and comfortable, you have to prepare today and lay the foundation of a comfortable future in retirement. The seed of that happy and comfortable future depends on your ability to reach your investment goals early in life. The need to defer gratification and continue to sow the seeds of greatness today will affect your retirement life in the future. This will, however, be dependent on your ability to stretch and expand your imagination. What you find today is the urge to make quick money without understanding the importance of gradual growth, proper investment, and patience.

The zeal and determination to achieve great outcome early in life when you are still young, strong, and full of energy would enable you to reach your goals and enjoy a happy and comfortable retirement life. You have to plan and work hard when you are still young with youthful energy. When you fail to work hard when you are still young, you will be compelled to work hard when you are old. That is why you see some people who started working hard early in life retire at forty or forty-five years, while others are just starting work at sixty.

That is why you need to plan early in life as you start that job, work hard and decide on what to do with your hard-earned income to secure your old age when the energy you have would have departed from you. Even as you have just started that job, start with the end in mind and be proactive. Looking ahead to the next ten, twenty, or thirty-five years, ask yourself, what will I be doing or be when I eventually retire? Knowing that the energy I have today would not be there for me at retirement, how can I utilize my hard-earned income that would come out of my hard work to enhance and ensure a happy and great retirement life? Once you have goals in place, going forward, you decide on how to focus on the direction of your future.

Before you retire, know that one of the most important aspects of your life after retirement is the skills you acquired while working. Self-development is the key to a happy and successful retirement life. What you acquired during your working life would influence your retirement life. Do not wait for the company or organization to train you; train yourself, most especially in the area of your interest or passion.

You will have to tackle the issues of life by acquiring knowledge. What you know will determine the extent you can go on the job. You can never go above your knowledge. Expand your knowledge by developing yourself personally. However, it is not just what you know but acting on what you know that matters.

Apply the Knowledge Acquired

Many people have knowledge, but they never apply it. The knowledge that is not applied is useless to the one who has it. What you don't know brings limitation into your life. The more ignorant you are, the more limited you will be and less value anybody can derive from you. Consequently, we will discuss in the course of reading this book, the issues of life that concern money, investment, success, setbacks, and comfort zone.

The price of success revolves around the actions required to achieve the progress you intend to make in life. You must be ready and determined to make the sacrifice required. Efforts must be made to concentrate and focus on that vision. You can create this vision in your mind by visualizing, creating a physical drawing of pictures and words that represent your dream of the future you envisaged for your life. Refer to this visual regularly, ideally every day. This should be the vision of why you are doing what you are doing. In the next ten years, what do you envisage to achieve in life? What you focus on in life and take action on will eventually become your reality.

For you to get to your future with success, there is a need to put what you have learned into action. Applying the knowledge will bring to reality the vision and dreams you have created. It enables you to achieve your vision, goal, and aspiration in life. Without applying the knowledge acquired, nothing happens. True knowledge is putting what you have learned into practice.

Most people live in the world of dreams and hopes but no action. For instance, many people dream of having an attractive, healthy body. So they dream of it but do not change their diet or their physical activities.

As the years go by, their weight goes up, and their health goes down. One day they go to the doctor, and the doctor does some tests. These tests are the feedback to the person for not taking action.

It takes aspiration, acquiring the necessary knowledge, and putting the knowledge into action to achieve your goals and dreams. Many people have great aspirations and even acquire the knowledge but get stuck there. They attend all the seminars, read all the books, and are online constantly researching. The problem is they never move on to applying the knowledge. Why? In most instances, it is because of fear. Fear of making mistakes, fear of losing money, fear of looking stupid, fear of people saying 'I told you.' It will not work. It is only when you apply the knowledge acquired that those fears will disappear. You have to believe in your ability if you intend to have a happy and comfortable life in retirement.

Focus on the Things That Make You Happy

Many people unfortunately focus on things that make them unhappy rather than happy, and soon their unhappiness grows. It also happens with our health. If a person is overweight, he/she tends to worry about gaining weight, rather than focus on his/her diet and how much he/she exercises. Or focus on what he/she dislikes and forget to focus on what he/she likes.

Your expectations will always come to pass if you take the necessary actions. Whatever you think is real eventually becomes your reality when you act and focus on the requirements. Your belief system affects your future and success in life.

Education is the key to human development and achievement. Personal development is the foundation that you need to progress in life. When it comes to true education, you need to personally continue to study, prepare, educate, train, and search for knowledge. Do not wait for your employers to train you. Any opportunity of learning should be utilized. The learning process must cut across the mental, emotional, physical, and spiritual parts of your whole being for it to have the desired impact.

Once the body, mind, spirit, and emotions understand the game and the process, you will never forget what has been taught.

One of the reasons lottery winners or sports stars often get broke a few years coming into millions is simply because they physically have the money but they have not changed emotionally, mentally, or spiritually. Consequently, the ability to utilize the money acquired in the lottery becomes a challenge and a spending spree becomes the order of the day. You, therefore, need to be sensitive to the urge to spend whenever your hard-earned income comes your way. Remember the source of your income will eventually come to an end one day.

For a person to mature and develop fully, he/she has to go beyond academic or mental development and go into personal development. This is because personal development is the education that strengthens the individual emotionally, physically, and spiritually. A truly intelligent person is the one who is in control of his/her mind, emotions, body, and spirit.

Focus on the positives of life, and concentrate on those things that make you happy. Face your passion and explore the work environment by making yourself relevant to the organization you have chosen to contribute to its success for you to have a happy and comfortable life in retirement.

Your Source of Income Will Not Last Forever

As you work and earn your income, remember that this source of income will not last forever. You will, one day, depart or leave that source, whether voluntarily or compulsorily, or old age will not give you the strength to work. While you are still strong and vibrant, you need to begin to plan ahead and be proactive by utilizing your time prudently. What do you do with the wee hours of your nights, weekends, vacations? How about using these hours to think and plan of launching great new ideas into actions that would produce solutions to the different problems that are around? Don't wait until you retire to think about and prepare your post retirement projects. If you are giving up work, then you need to find a replacement for what you have lost.

Those you work with and relations around you will usually be sources of information regarding what to do in retirement. Some intentionally give you information that will assist you, while others give you advice as a result of personal care and concern. Normally, colleagues and family members offer different advice in a bid to add value or deliberately, in some cases, to distract you, as the case may be. Eventually, one is exposed to fear in one way or the other. For you to excel, enjoy your future and eventually have a happy and comfortable life in retirement. There is, therefore, the need to avoid all forms of free advice and information that may create fear. The fear of failure in terms of the choices you make concerning your life after retirement must be checked. Avoid free advice from colleagues and family friends.

In the next chapter, the working class is presented with the need to prepare early for a happy and comfortable life in retirement. The way to identify individual passion and centre one's retirement in order to

Chapter 3
THE WORKING CLASS

People with purpose are powerhouses of possibilities. Be expectant and you will give birth to a great future. The greatest discovery any man can make, is the purpose they have been born for and then to pursue it with a passion.

—Peter Sinclair

When the life of the working class in society and their life after retirement is examined, it is usually expected that their standard of living will be better at retirement if they had pursued their purpose with passion during their youthful working years. However, it is not usually the same with those who did not. The working classes in our society today are faced with a lot of challenges.

A lot of those working and almost on their way to retirement who did not consider early preparation for retirement a priority are often affected. The working life of an individual can be demanding and full of challenges due to the magnitude of changes in the work environment. Having spent a greater part of their life working, their mindset and manner of behaviour would have been affected by the work environment. The idea of planning and preparing for retirement during their working life usually does not make sense even when the signs are obviously visible.

The culture of the organization has a great effect on the life of its workers. As a worker, you must have been influenced by the corporate culture of the organization. You have been groomed to behave the way your organization has directed your path through the different rules and regulations guiding your duties in the workplace. It becomes a normal routine to get up early in the morning to prepare for work and dress in the office style of work.

You are made to imbibe the culture of your organization consciously or unconsciously over the years. Letting work go may not be easy, considering the fact that work is such an important part of your life. It should not come as a surprise that leaving it behind would have a great emotional and psychological shock on you. There is, therefore, a need to prepare emotionally, psychologically, and financially and to centre your retirement on your passion in order to enjoy a happy and comfortable life in retirement.

Prepare Emotionally

Once you approach your retirement, the tendency is that you may start to think that it is too late to plan for retirement. This state of mind usually brings about emotional impact on you leaving that job. Hence, there is a need to practically start preparing for retirement and when you will eventually retire. It is not late to prepare. What is important is to have confidence in your ability and bear in mind that it is better to be late than never, as an old saying goes. At this stage, as I said earlier, you have to change, control, and expand your realities. You have to have a new mindset of a reality of a possible positive future that awaits you.

A new mindset of positive possibility that would enable you to expand your imagination and think outside the box is necessary for a happy, successful, and comfortable life in retirement. That normal corporate life you are used to will have to change. For you to prepare for retirement while working can be a challenge. You may have to anticipate and imbibe change, which is a constant.

In preparing for retirement, a lot of things will have to change in your working life. You have to expect that during retirement, the relationship you had with your colleagues, the way you related to them, would not be the same, and even at the family level, your role at home may have to change as you eventually retire. At retirement, there is a change from having nice offices, a steady pay cheque, and everything paid by the company or organization to a world where you pay for everything, including paper clips, and every little thing that you can imagine.

All these changes will have an emotional impact on you. Consequently, you may have to accept the emotional impacts that are usually devastating. This is usually more devastating on those whose retirement came suddenly. The size of your house, the number of cars, moving near relatives, moving to a new location, and the type of friends you intend to keep, must be considered before you retire. Transiting from working life to retirement can have a serious impact on the life of an individual who is not prepared for the life after work. What usually brings joy to some would bring sadness to others.

If you are of the working class engaged in hard work and those who may be on their way out of the job environment, it is imperative that you look ahead into the future from where you are. What type of retirement life do you intend to live after you leave that job? Where do you intend to spend the rest of your life, and what type of friends and environment do you wish to stay with? Do you intend to engage in working life after your retirement? What type of investment do you intend to put your savings and retirement income into? Adequate knowledge about investment is required. Early preparation for retirement and learning how to manage your retirement are necessary requirements for the person who intends to have a happy and comfortable life in retirement.

For your retirement life to be happy and comfortable, there is also a need to decide on what you intend to do during retirement. While researching this book, I discovered that a lot of people do not intend to do anything during their retirement, while some do not know what they would be doing during their retirement. Very few actually have an idea of what they intend to do when their working days are over. Well, the truth is those who prepare early for retirement, most of the time, are those who are emotionally happy and comfortable at retirement.

Those who did not prepare at all for retirement are those who get into retirement traumatized as their transition from work to retirement often become rough. That is why it is recommended that you prepare for retirement emotionally even if you are not sure of what you will be doing at retirement. The interesting aspect is that in retirement, you have the freedom to do whatever you want. If you want to relax, relax. If you want to keep working, keep working; the choice is yours. However, regardless of what you choose, you still need to prepare on how to go about your retirement in a positive way.

Prepare Psychologically

The reality of life concerning your job must be understood. One day you will lose your job that you started some time ago, either by choice or by force! Consequently, you have to prepare yourself psychologically. The reality of leaving that job will have a psychological impact on you. One day you will have to go away from that workplace you have been going to and coming from for no matter how long it has taken you. In life, the truth is everything that has a start has an end. There is a day to begin and a day to end, a day to be born and a day to die. Just as there is death in life, there is retirement in the workplace. Those who begin with the end in mind live the highest quality of life in retirement.

The greatest liberation any human can ever experience lies on the realization that fears should not hold him/her back. The same way that dying makes living exciting, the same way the thought of the day you will lose your job should make you spend the time you currently have wisely.

Retirement naturally should be expected in every worker's life. Life is in stages. When you are born, when you get to school for your studies, when you start your first paying job, when you get experience, when you get promoted, and the day you lose that job by virtue of age or completion of years of service. Most people do not think about retirement until it's too late or when they are already fifty or approaching sixty. Preparing for retirement when you are already old or retired can be traumatic. Those who refuse to prepare early for this important phase of their working life would face the stress of difficulties in their old age during retirement.

The challenges of transiting from working life to retirement can be traumatic and shocking. Retirement requires personal adjustment as the workplace and the home environment are two distinct places that must be treated differently. The working life is practically different from that of retirement. When you discuss retirement with those who have retired, they will confirm that life after retirement is different from the working time. Almost all the retired people I talked to were united in their views on the difference of their lives in retirement and their working times. You, therefore, need to prepare psychologically if you want a happy and comfortable life in retirement.

Prepare Financially

In retirement, you will definitely need money to do whatever you have chosen to do in a comfortable way. A lot of people retire without proper preparation and end up traumatized due to the challenges that go with retirement. Many retire and attempt to live on a lot less because they underestimated their standard of living. I have heard of general managers, senior managers, and directors who lived in big houses and drove the flashiest cars ended up as high-class beggars and mere social and political commentators. Why? Because while they were on their jobs, they thought erroneously that it would last forever. They did not know that the end was nearer than farther. While they carried buckets, they considered the act of stooping to build pipes too low for them. Some of them left their jobs with huge bank balances, but the entrepreneurial technique, which has no respect for years of experience, dealt them a knock out in the early rounds of their ventures.

You have to prepare for the retirement life that is ahead and will surely come sooner than you thought. Start exposing yourself and getting yourself set for when you will lose your job. Mark my words, the first showers of the great storms are all that we have seen; many who are comfortable today will be beggars tomorrow if they do not prepare for the end today. Many who are not developing their skills today will be slaves tomorrow, and many who have ill-gotten money today will be needy tomorrow if they did not change their ways. The storm is coming; let he who is wise join the company of Noah in the Ark of deliverance that is being built and let the fools scorn and laugh.

The truth is, if you are reading this book in your forties or fifties, then you need to be thinking very hard about your financial preparations for your retirement and how you intend to treat your money matters during your retirement, as retirement is closer than you will like to think. You also need to know that retirement will last longer for you than it did for your parents. Reliable and latest research in the US suggests that around 50 per cent of fifty-year-olds will live until they are at least ninety years old. You, therefore, need to make preparations for a lengthy retirement life or be prepared to work longer in your old age.

In life, as you have the opportunity to be a worker, this period of your life should be very important to you because you have the opportunity, strength, youthfulness, and energy to work hard to achieve the targets set by your employers and those you set for yourself. Never waste any part of your working life. Never waste the opportunities that come your way. The choices you make at this stage of your life will determine the happiness, comfort, or otherwise of your retirement. At retirement, that energy and vibrancy begin to fade away. Prepare early at this stage when your youthful energy is still available for you to enjoy your retirement life.

What you do with your time now will shape what you do with your time when your working days are over. Every day, you choose what to do with your time, and every day, you choose what information you put into your brain. You can choose to watch television all day long, read inspirational books, attend seminars to become financially educated, or do nothing at all. You can decide to sit and wait for retirement or choose to prepare and enjoy a happy and comfortable life in retirement. The choices you make today will detect and determine the happiness, comfort, or otherwise of your retirement. What you do with your working life will affect your retirement life. The opportunities you utilize positively today will contribute positively to your retirement life when your working days are over. Make every effort to make proper use of your working days so as to have a happy and comfortable life in retirement.

Your habits have the potential to make or mar you. Bad habits affect you and the people around you negatively. The ability to maintain great habits would dictate the happiness and comfort of your life in retirement. What you continuously repeat becomes your habit. Choose good habits to have a wonderful life, both at work and in retirement. The routine of the workplace is different from that of retirement. The good routine that enhances your health will contribute to the happiness and comfort of your retirement life. The things that make life happy and comfortable are usually those activities that are difficult and painful in the first instance, but with determination and focus, the benefits associated with these activities will normally result in the comfort that is obtained at the end of the exercise.

Planning for retirement begins with a plan. The plan must have a time limit that has an end or exit strategy. If you do not plan for retirement, you are planning to work all your life. Planning to work hard all your life is a poor plan. When you work hard today and have nothing set aside for tomorrow, you are exposing yourself to a hard life when you are old and retired. Preparing for retirement begins with the right mindset, the right words, and the right plan. When you have that plan, the action steps are easy. You have to plan for retirement now if you want to have a happy and rewarding retirement. You have to write down the goal, create a plan, and focus on the idea.

Do not think your retirement is too far ahead. Check around and be sensitive to the changes that are taking place. You have probably noticed that the years are running fast and seem to spin round faster as you get older, and so you will have realized that retirement is closer than you will like to think. Also, do not be surprised by the fact that retirement probably will last longer for you than it did for your parents.

You will have to make the right choices. Start the preparation right now if you have not begun to take actions for a lengthy retirement, or be prepared to work longer. As you reach your mid-forties, you should be thinking of the different ways of utilizing your hard-earned income into the asset that would bring cash flow into your system so that your retirement life will be happy and comfortable.

At retirement, you will require good health to enjoy your retirement. Money or not, no one wants to waste his retirement sitting in a hospital bed. Your health is, therefore, important, and consequently, you need to develop good health habits that will enhance your retirement life. Do not ignore your health, as it is not wise to use your retirement funds on treatment.

For your retirement life to be happy and comfortable and your investment to be the panacea for a guaranteed future, you must plan early for your retirement. For your financial independence to be sustained, you must identify your financial goals, write them down, prepare a plan of action, and continue to do something every day that would move you towards the achievement of a happy and comfortable life in retirement.

Centre Your Retirement on Your Passion

When it comes to retirement and what to do during retirement, from the findings of the research of this book, those who usually enjoy their retirement are those who prepare for retirement and centre their retirement on their passion. If your passion is sports, plan your retirement around it. Whatever your passion, plan and prepare your retirement around it because that is the area that will bring satisfaction to you. That is why Peter Sinclair emphatically stated, 'People with purpose are powerhouses of possibilities. Be expectant and you will give birth to a great future. The greatest discovery any man can make, is the purpose they have been born for and then to pursue it with a passion.'

When you, therefore, pursue the business venture(s) you identify through your work as you prepare for retirement with passion, you would discover that the transition from work to retirement becomes seamless. What do you want to do during retirement? Start planning for it. What is your passion? Build your retirement around your passion. Is it golf, sports, travelling, or service to humanity or religious commitments? Or is it business or investment? Whatever your passion, pursue it. Decide on the type of activity you intend to engage in during your retirement while you are still working. If you want to be an entrepreneur, it might be a good idea to study the lives of entrepreneurs and the different types of businesses they created.

The problem with this group of people who did not prepare and centre their retirement on their passion is that they find it difficult to identify what they intend to do during that period of their life. It is, therefore, advisable to identify your passion and decide on what to do during retirement with your passion in mind. When you set or choose your retirement engagements based on your passion, you will discover that where your passion is, there is happiness, and even without payment, you will be willing to engage yourself in activities that affect your passion effortlessly.

There are, therefore, different ways of identifying your passion and areas of activities that will make your retirement happy and comfortable. These ways are not limited to the ones written below. You may explore other ways that you find interesting.

> 1. *Childhood or early days' experience.* One of the ways to find your passion is to reflect back on your childhood days and think of those things that you liked. What were those activities that took your time, which you enjoyed the most whenever you engaged in them? In terms of games, plays, and handicrafts, what took your time that you found exciting to the extent that you had to be called to eat and you would feel you were being disturbed? You need to check on such activities; they could be your areas of passion in which you could develop various ideas in retirement.

> 2. *Past and present dreams' experience.* Another way of identifying your passion is to check your dreams. Oftentimes your dreams are functions of your innermost passion. Those things that occupy your thoughts are usually the deep-seated ideas that you care for and, hence, their manifestation in the form of dreams. When you follow your dreams during your retirement, there is usually fulfilment when those dreams occupy you upon retirement. What are those dreams that you dreamt when you started work? Have you fulfilled all your dreams? The unfulfilled dreams could be areas that you could explore to make your retirement life happy and fully engaged. Planning your retirement with these dreams in mind will make your retirement activities fulfilling.

> 3. *Comments from people around you.* The best way to identify your passion and plan your retirement around it is to consider the

comments of the people around you. Whenever you perform activities or function at your work place, listen to the comments made by your colleagues and superiors. You have to be sensitive to the comments that are made concerning those activities that have to do with your competences. Your areas of passion are those things you love and enjoy doing that people around you would always be surprised as to how you are able to perform such a feat seamlessly. To them, you are naturally endowed with that ability to the extent that they are amazed as to how you are able to perform such activity. 'How did you do it?' 'You are excellent in this area, and I wonder how you did it.' 'Wow! This is wonderful!' You need to check such comments, as they may be pointers to your passion that you could dwell on during your retirement.

4. *Past work experience.* In planning and preparing for your retirement, there may be a need to consider your wealth of experience you have gathered over the years that could be useful to you during your retirement. This is a key for those who normally intend to set up their business. Those who intend to be consultants or engage in part-time work have to rely on their work experience. The experience you gathered over the years could be an asset if you want to set up your business in retirement. The routine and culture of the organization you worked for all these years could be the basis upon which you could set up your business that could make your retirement happy and comfortable.

5. *The problems of society's experience.* The problems that exist in the society could be the basis upon which your passion may be built on. Your passion may be to solve a particular problem that exists in the society during your retirement. When you have such a passion and you prepare your retirement around that, you will discover that your retirement will be interesting. Some retired people who are passionate in giving back to society during their retirement usually end up setting non-profit organizations that are beneficial to society and their retirement.

6. *The still little voice experience.* Above all these factors is the still

little voice that keeps on prompting you each time you decide to act. The problem is we are usually not sensitive and attentive to this very important little voice that keeps drawing our attention to the issues of life anytime we are about to take a decision. Your retirement is another great stage in your life, and whatever you intend to do during this stage of your life requires that you listen to the prompting of your maker. Whatever you intend to do during your retirement will be dependent on the prompting of the Holy Spirit for those who believe in God. Find your inspiration from your maker, and your retirement will be happy and comfortable.

When you identify your passion, there is a need to look ahead and prepare early for your retirement. Have you thought of the most important issues of life that you will face at retirement? If you have not started yet, why not set some time apart when you will have a quiet time to tackle the preparation as a project? You can start by carrying out a financial review. Find out your net worth. What your pension will be worth at retirement. What you will require to live on in retirement. Will you require relocation or stay where you are? You have to do some detailed research into the likely benefits and costs of your retirement plan. There is a need to get a clear idea of what kind of things will make you feel happy, fulfilled, and successful.

In the next chapter, retired people and what they need to do to have a happy and comfortable life are discussed. The different aspects of retirement and the need to have a positive mindset in tackling challenges at retirement are emphasized.

Chapter 4
THE RETIRED

Today, retirees need more financial resources at retirement and more sophisticated ways of building assets than were differed by the pension plans of the Industrial Age.

—Robert T. Kiyosaki

Whenever retirement is mentioned, the first thing that comes to mind is life during retirement. Those who are retired are often seen as senior citizens who have contributed their youthful lives to society and are expected to plough back what they had given society into the comfort of their retirement. However, most of those senior citizens are confronted with all sorts of challenges and hardships due to several factors, ranging from their lack of early planning for retirement to faulty functionality of their pensions. Corruption has also contributed to the hard conditions of these senior citizens, who had placed their retirement on these pension plans only to be told that their hard-earned income has been wiped out by corruption. Also changes in the financial environment and policies of government would have affected their envisaged future. High inflation rate could make the value of their savings worthless after many years. These unforeseen circumstances could influence the plans that these senior citizens would have put in place.

Retirement life is not a death sentence but another stage in the lives of those who have tested the busy working life where stress and deadlines were the order of the day. The transition from the working life to retirement can be hectic and traumatizing if plans had not been put in place from the first instance. Emotionally, psychologically, and financially, retirement has its impact. Whether you prepared for retirement or not, once you are retired, you will have to confront the issues of life. This includes the issues of money, investment, success, setbacks or failures, and the impact of the comfort zone.

For you who are already retired, I intend to share with you what I have discovered from your retired colleagues during the course of writing this book. The issues that we intend to discuss in this chapter cut across the entire divide. While writing on retirement and knowing that I am still working, initially, I felt my ideas would have to wait until such a time I would retire and gather enough experience on retirement matters before I publish this book. I felt challenged. However, the urge to share my discoveries with all encouraged me to proceed. It gave me a difficult task and brought out the need to research more on the subject matter. However, I discovered that the more I researched, the more there was the need to share my ideas with those who would benefit from this work. In fact, I came to realize that each time I met any retired person, most of them were keen to listen to the issues of life regarding money, investment, success, setbacks, and the impact of the comfort zone.

While I was struggling to put the issues of life across to the retired people, I felt uncomfortable; however, the responses I received encouraged me to go ahead with the work you are reading today. Almost all the retired people I talked with confirmed that these issues of life are worth discussing as they affect the preparation for retirement. Preparing for retirement in good time affects your retirement life as retirement has the tendency of changing your perception of the new person you are now and also change other people's perception about you.

Surplus Time

One of the hardest things about being in retirement, according to those who have retired, is the challenge of having nothing to do. After years of schooling, classroom studies, tests, meetings, and deadlines at work, one is truly conditioned to get up and rush off to do something. Just before retiring, one may actually start hating the pressure or worry of work. However, immediately one retires, you discover you are restless, even continue to wake up early, only to realize that you had no plans for the day. In fact, one of my senior colleagues who had retired woke up on his first day in retirement and dressed up on his favourite suit as usual and was waiting for his driver to take him to the office, only to be reminded that his retirement has commenced.

At retirement, you now have the time to think on those ideas and projects you could not execute due to the needs and pressures from the workplace. You now have the time to fulfil your ambitions as you no longer have to get up at a particular time to go to work, dress in work clothes, and face the relentless pressure of work deadlines or deal with office politics. The freedom acquired as a result of retirement could be exciting and, at the same time, be traumatic.

Due to this belief of having surplus time during retirement, nowadays, a lot of people often start their retirement with a sense of excitement and a feeling of starting a honeymoon. This initial period of honeymoon is the time during which the recently retired feel that they have been given an extended holiday. They are excited and start off by attending to all the things they were unable to do or those things they have wanted to do but could not due to pressure of work. They start these things with great zeal and excitement, only to discover that the holiday is not ending.

This challenge, if not addressed, usually leads to depression and a feeling of dejection. It could also lead to creativity for those who decide to utilize this window as an opportunity to think through to create value. In his book Retire Young and Retire Rich, Robert Kiyosaki describes how he utilized the first year of his retirement to think and reflect on his life to write the Rich Dad, Poor Dad book that became a best seller. The surplus time during retirement could, therefore, be utilized for the achievement of unfulfilled dreams, projects, and passionable ventures that could make retirement happy and comfortable. If you can utilize this available time to reflect on your past with the aim of adding value to yourself and the society by harnessing those ideas and aspirations you had while working, and those experiences you gathered when you were contributing to the success of your organization, your retirement will be happy and comfortable. You will discover that doing what you enjoy will enhance your retirement and make life comfortable.

Actually, the best thing about retirement is that it gives you a chance to start life all over again. You will have the chance to reflect on the past and take steps that will affect your future, which is the other half and final lap of your life. You will learn to appreciate life even if it was hectic, stressful, and filled with problems. Whatever your state of life in the present, take a moment to appreciate it because tomorrow, it will only be a memory.

One problem many retired people face is that they have more time to read dailies and watch news unfolding on the television and Internet. This can expose you to panics and scary stories. Consequently, there is need to organize and prioritize the method and manner of information you assimilate during your retirement. Select the information that will motivate and encourage you. Inspirational materials and educational inputs into your system will activate your creative mind. You will be filled with value and virtue that will enhance your ability to pursue your passion. At retirement, the best thing to do is to follow one's passion. You have to engage in those things that usually excited you and made you happy when you were younger, during your working days. Those activities you enjoyed are the things that will make your retirement happy and comfortable.

Leaving Behind a Comfortable Life

The challenges of those retired are beyond having nothing to do while on retirement. Leaving behind a comfortable habit of receiving salaries every month, the impact of having been used to a routine of going to work every day, a formal organized daily routine, for a life of endless staying at home without deadlines and meetings can be challenging. Retirement is a life of an individual thinking alone, which is different from teamwork with colleagues.

As I mentioned earlier, times have changed. The retirement life of the past is different from that of today. Life expectancy has equally changed. You are likely expected to stay alive longer than your parents due to improved medical facilities. Consequently, you require more money and resources to sustain this long life that you will enjoy during retirement. That is why Robert Kiyosaki in his book, Retire Young and Retire Rich stated, 'Today, retirees need more financial resources at retirement and more sophisticated ways of building assets than were differed by the pension plans of the Industrial Age.'

Despite all said and done, retirement is neither a death sentence nor a period of mourning. It is a new phase of life that calls for celebration for having contributed positively to society and humanity. It is a mature phase that requires a new strategy and approach. If you are retired, and most probably you did not plan early for retirement or if your retirement came unprepared, there is no need to panic as all is not lost. Whichever state of mind you are in, the reality of life is that retirement is real and must be treated with the facts of today.

Adjustment Time

When you were working, you were under the control of your employers. No wonder most retired people feel life after retirement is freedom and equate one's working life to corporate slavery since you were directed, influenced, controlled, and subjected to the rules and regulations of your organization.

To be set free from the corporate slavery will make you a different person, and consequently, there may be the need to adjust from a life of restriction to that of freedom. Many retired people go through a significant trauma in the transition to retirement, having spent a better part of their lives in the work environment. This is because the early stages of retirement can be traumatic, most especially when the retirement meets you unprepared.

Although some may discover on the first day of their retirement that they are now on holiday for the rest of their lives, others will feel a traumatic effect as they feel work was such an important part of their lives, and leaving it behind for a new life requires serious adjustment. With this confusion in the mindset of the retired person, there is a need for mindset adjustment.

This is also a period when the bulk of the retirement incomes are available, lavishly and uncontrollably spent by those who do not have plans. You find emotional buying and venturing into ventures that come their way without proper investigations. As a retired person, you need to control your spending emotions and be sensitive to those who will bring new ideas to the ways you should spend or utilize your retirement resources. This is the period you require professionals to articulate and advice on different aspects of what you intend to do.

For you to adjust financially, most of the retired people I talked to concluded that financial adjustment is necessary as you have to be prepared to cut your expenditure to fit your new retirement income. To adjust financially, some retired people do engage in part-time jobs. The need to keep working part-time probably will increase their income. Some become consultants, utilizing their vast experience to keep them busy. Other retired people decide to start their business. Engaging in business, you have to think very carefully before risking your retirement savings on a business venture or engaging in your own business outfit. This will be discussed in detail in other chapters of this book as part of the issues of life.

Retirement requires personal adjustment as the workplace and the home environment are two distinct places that must be treated differently. The work environment, being a formal set-up with a well-defined routine aimed at achieving results that are based on deadlines, would have had a tremendous impact on the life of anyone who has experienced the work environment. For you to adjust from a working life to retirement, you may have to establish a new routine. This new routine may have an impact on your activities. In creating a new routine, care must be taken to avoid routines that will be hazardous to your health. A routine that does not take care of your emotional, psychological, and physical life should be avoided.

The Better Phase of Life

In the retirement stage, you are now in the better half of your life. You are older, wiser, smarter, and less reckless. It is no longer life dictated by the wishes of your parents, teachers, friends, or employers. The other half of your life has begun, and this time is a time that will be on your own terms and conditions. You are totally in charge of your life going forward, and consequently, all efforts should be geared towards your passion—those activities you enjoy and love doing without being paid.

It gives you a chance to start your life all over without much interference by others. As stated earlier, it is true that you cannot change your past, but you have the ability to correct the mistakes and the opinions of your past and take positive choices that will change your future. There may be the need to take time and look at the possibilities that are available. Rediscover yourself and get into activities that bring excitement to you. Your future depends on the choices you make at this stage of your life.

It will be the best time to talk about how you intend to manage your new life that is free and devoid of control. You may have to think about how your home would accommodate you spending much more time in it. You may also need to think about how you want to prioritize your time for those things you value. Your retirement will have a great impact on your lifestyle and those around you. It will change a lot of things in your life, and consequently, it is worth thinking about whether you are considering changing your lifestyle in retirement or other changes that could occur in your life.

With increasing life expectancies, most retired people have to plan for a longer time to maintain a decent standard of living into their eighties. This means that most retired people have to invest for the long term, and there are no truly safe options to managing your investment. Make sure you enjoy it. In fact, retirement should be the best time in one's life and should be adequately enjoyed. This was properly expressed by Nic Peeling in his book Brilliant Retirement: 'Retirement should be the best time of your life, so make sure you enjoy it.'

Periodically Review Your Retirement

Retirement is not a death sentence but a new phase of life. From the retired people I talked to, it is clear that in this phase of your retirement, you have the freedom of choice. You decide whatever you choose to do. If you want to enjoy a happy and comfortable life in retirement, it is essential that you periodically review your retirement. Consequently, there is a need to always review the retirement journey to check the choices you made, whether they are still on course or not. What is your retirement vision? Have you achieved it? What are your retirement missions, plans, goals, and objectives?

The truth is whatever you think about and talk about always grows. The more you think about yourself as healthy and well, the better your body will be. The more you think of prosperity, abundance, and success, the more of these things you will bring into your life. The more you think of the good fortune you have had, the more good fortune will come your way. The more you think of a positive, happy, and comfortable retirement life, the better and happier your retirement life will be.

In the same vein, the more you think about your indigestion or your rheumatism, the worse it becomes. The more you think of lack and of bad times, the worse your business will be. Also, the more you think about grievances or injustices that you have suffered, the more such trials will you continue to receive. The same way, the more you think of a negative retirement life, the worse your retirement will be.

You therefore need to be sensitive to the things you think and talk about all the times. Concentrate on the positive part of your retirement, and as much as possible, avoid those things that you do not want to happen to you. That is why emphasis should be made on issues of life that will make your retirement happy and comfortable.

Develop a Positive Mindset

The retirement life is a unique phase in the life of the retiree. You will encounter different challenges while on retirement. However, your attitude to these challenges will determine how happy you will be. The best approach that will give you a happy and comfortable life in retirement is the maintenance of a positive mindset whenever you come across challenges or setbacks. Those who approach life challenges with a positive mindset usually adapt to different aspects of living with calmness. They are people who prepare for and accept change. Being optimistic in approach will enable you to see issues in a more positive manner, whatever situation you find yourself.

Where are you with regards to your family life and relationships? With your retirement status, you will be better off and happy if you enhance your family relationships and develop a new social network of friends that you will network with as your former colleagues will not be there for you. To have a happy and comfortable life in retirement, there is need to connect with new friends that would enhance your new personality.

What about health and fitness? While you were working, your schedule of waking up to go to work would have prevented you from adhering to healthy routines. In retirement, you now have the opportunity to develop a good and healthy routine. The time to engage in exercises that will improve your health is now.

What about your will? Is it still valid? You must continually ask these important questions in order to check your retirement journey. What are the things that you cherish and intend to pursue in your retirement? Identify and continue to think over these things.

There are basically two factors that could contribute to a happy and comfortable life in retirement. The first is the psychological factors like your state of mind. How positive you are will affect your retirement life. How optimistic you are will equally affect your retirement. Your relationship can determine how happy and comfortable your retirement life will be. The way you update your reality of the world and the level of your networking could detect the level of your happiness and comfort of your retirement.

The second is the practical factors, which are the issues of life that includes money, investment, success, setbacks, and the comfort zone. These factors are discussed in detail in subsequent chapters.

In the chapter, one of the issues of life, money, is discussed. For you to enjoy a happy and comfortable life in your retirement, there is need to understand the fundamentals of money, which is the oxygen of investment. The different ways people go to get money and the right ways to handle it are discussed to enhance your retirement life.

Chapter 5
Money Matters

Money won't make you rich because a man who is poor in spirit is poor altogether, even when he has a lot of money in his pocket. Money without the wealth of the soul is equalled to a compilation of sorrows and regrets. Only God enriches without adding sorrow to it.

—Sunday Adelaja

Whenever the aspect of money matters is discussed, the greatest concern of most retired people and which often causes the most angst is the matter of money. This mostly has to do with the concern about whether the individual will be able to live on a reduced income and whether he or she can protect that income and savings from the ravages of inflation. This concern is usually ignored by most workers until it is virtually late, as emphasis is placed on other important aspects of life.

Another area of great concern has to do with the lack of understanding of the matters of money. Even when you have toiled, working hard for years, oftentimes you discover that due to lack of understanding, this hard-earned money ends up being wrongly applied in ventures that could consume such efforts. That is why in most societies today, the greatest fear is not terrorism but running out of money during retirement. Having a great knowledge of the principles and laws of money often differentiates those who become rich and have the ability to sustain such wealth to a particular level in their retirement.

In money matters, you have to be prepared to expand your knowledge of the principles of money and sources of income to enable you to cope with your expenditure that will fit your new retirement status and make your retirement happy and comfortable. This some retired people do by engaging in part-time jobs, becoming consultants or operating their own business. You should, however, not put your eggs in the same basket whenever you decide to invest. It is worth understanding that some of your investments will do better than others, and as a result, you need to review your different portfolios as you progress.

Money is a sensitive and emotional topic that we always shy away from its discussion. However, you must be able to control your emotions to have control over your money. Your emotions have to do with your soul. The health of your soul detects the state of your emotion. That is why Sunday Adelaja, in his book Money Can't Make You Rich, states, 'Money won't make you rich because a man who is poor in spirit is poor altogether, even when he has a lot of money in his pocket. Only God enriches without adding sorrow to it.' Incidentally, since money is an emotional issue, those who have been able to overcome its emotional tendency, have contributed to most of the successes and the sustainable wealth of the society in human history, and hence, they have the happiest and most comfortable life in retirement.

The importance of money cannot be overemphasized as most of our modern discoveries wouldn't have been possible without the availability of money. Whether you are retired or not, you need money to survive. Whether you invest or not, you still need money to function in your activities. Whether you are rich or poor, you require money to carry out your activities. Whether you are in the city or village, you desire money to meet your needs. Whatever your religion, you need money to perform your religious activities effectively. Whether you succeed or fail, you require money to move forward. When it comes to the issue of money, there is no south, there is no north, and there is no west or east. Money is a unifying force.

We have seen in many societies today that individuals accumulate money that is meant for the generality of the society for their selfish desires. Those you do not expect will disappoint you will eventually do so when it comes to the issue of money. You never can tell who can be trusted with money because of the sensitivity of money.

Many relationships have been destroyed because of money acquired without the wealth of the soul, as clearly stated by Sunday Adelaja: 'Money without the wealth of the soul is equalto a compilation of sorrows and regrets.' You see two brothers fighting to the extent of destroying each other because of money. Marriages are dissolved because of money. You find great men of God with powerful ministries destroyed because of money. Nations fight nations because of the interest that is traced to money through investment. Corruption is everywhere because of the need to accumulate more money by selfish individuals and organizations.

There is an aspect of money that you need to know as you start that job or prepare for your retirement or embark on your retirement. This aspect is the lack of the diminishing marginal utility of money. All other commodities have a diminishing return as you acquire and use them, but money does not. By this, I mean money is the only commodity on earth that has this attribute: the more you get it, the more you want to get. Consequently, there is the tendency to be selfish if one is not careful. For instance, when you are hungry and you are given a plate of food. The tendency is that your first spoon would be sweeter than the last, and of course, the moment your stomach is filled, any attempt to go beyond that would result in vomiting. That means that you can get to the point where you will no longer need this food. This is what is lacking when it comes to the accumulation of money.

What you find is some people have this tendency: the more they get money, the more they want to get it. There is no point in the lives of most men wherein they dislike the need to have additional money. That is why you find some people accumulating money without looking back; as they get money, that urge to get more continues into infinity. Hence, the corrupt tendencies set in. Knowing that money is the only commodity on earth that does not have diminishing marginal utility, it calls for caution and carefulness in the ways we acquire and handle it in our bid to acquire it for better performance and a happy and comfortable life in retirement.

While you prepare for your future and eventual retirement, the other aspect of money I want us to look at is the idea people have whenever money is not yet available. You will discover that your desires and wants before you acquire money would always appear to be different from the ones that come into your system when money eventually comes. The most brilliant ideas surface when you do not have money. The ideas that the mind wants will always occupy you, and most of the time, plans are quickly drafted. However, the moment money comes into your system, different and wild ideas will immediately start occupying the mind. At this moment, it takes a strong mind to stick to the previous ideas. Thereafter, what happens is the weak mind will abandon the previous idea and jump into carrying out the recent ones, only to discover that the wrong ideas have been adopted. Consequently, different people go into different ways and means to acquire money. How you acquire money influences the way you utilize it. If you acquire money from the right source, it brings along with it blessings.

Money is seen as the oxygen of investment that is required for you to succeed and effectively manage your retirement. You also need to know that apart from being the oxygen of investment, money is a game—and a very important one, for that matter—in the field of investment. If you know the rules, you win; if you don't know the rules, you lose. That is why you see those who succeed in investment continually seek knowledge in the field of investment.

The successful people in the society have continued to acquire abundant knowledge of the game of money, and consequently, they use money according to the rules and in ways that bring profit and returns on their investment. The end result is financial independence, happiness, and success while working during retirement.

Just as the natural law does not discriminate, money does not. Whether you are working or retired, tall or short, white or black, an individual or organization, if you treat money according to the rules, you will win; otherwise, you will lose. The foundation of your financial success while in retirement depends on the way you play the game. No wonder you discover that money vanishes from the hands of those who mishandle it due to leakages that exist in terms of their lack of planning whenever purchases are made

Furthermore, in your workplace, while preparing for your retirement or during retirement, you need to also know that money is blind and goes to those who know how to handle it prudently. The fact is, money likes staying and multiplying in the hands of those who can send it on duty to work for them. Money runs away from those who are not aware of the ways to engage it into different active duties. The moment you spend money, it runs away from you because money spent does not return, but money invested not only returns but also brings additional money back to those who invest it.

It is often said that the love of money is the root of all evil. Most of the time, this Bible verse is often misquoted and interpreted wrongly to mean money is the root of all evil. Obviously, the correct interpretation of the verse is if you make money your god and you pursue affluence to the exclusion of other values, you lose out. Truly, anyone who makes money and becomes financially independent but ignores his emotional and spiritual pursuit is simply a bankrupt soul.

The truth is, money can be the root of your success when sought for and utilized properly. Money can certainly make life easier, more comfortable, and more secure in retirement. It can open more doors, take you to places you have never been, and allow you to meet people you would otherwise never have met. But the bad news is that it cannot buy you happiness. As clearly stated by Robert G. Allen, 'Money may not buy you happiness, but it surely helps one look for it in more interesting places.' Money is the oxygen and current of investment; there is a need to understand other aspects of money that ordinarily we often ignore. In the same manner, money cannot make you rich, but the principles and ways of getting money can. If you are aware of the principles of making money, even when you have no money in your possession while in retirement, you can still have a meaningful and happy retirement life.

Do you know why the Good Samaritan was referred to in the Bible and is being recognized today? It was because he had the intention and also had the money that he used in taking the sick man to the hospital. Had it been that he had only the intention to assist but no money with him, do you think the impact of his adventure would have been recorded to give any meaning? Definitely, I can say, not at all. But because he had the money, he was able to take this man to the hospital, deposit money, and give the necessary instructions to the hospital officials to take care of the patient. He also instructed the hospital to keep the record so that when he came back, he would make the reimbursement.

Many people have therefore concluded that if you have more money, you are rich and successful. This is a wrong impression. The truth is being truly rich and successful in life means having many more important things than just having money.

A lot of people I talked to while researching for this book worried because they did not know how long they would live and, hence, found it difficult and hard to plan for their old age. For those just starting work, there is a need to learn the principles of money, how to apply your hard-earned money in ventures that would make your money grow while you progress in your career.

If you are already working or about to retire, you also need to understand the rules of money. You have to be cautious with the way you handle what you work hard for to avoid the trap of losing it to fraudsters, predators, and bad investments while you prepare for your retirement. For those already retired, you also have to be cautious in handling your savings and pension. You must handle your money cautiously for at least the first year of retirement; give room for stability, both psychologically and practically, in the new status—retirement.

Different Ways of Acquiring Money

It is now clear that money obviously plays an important role in investment and other areas of our existence. It also plays an important role during your working and retirement life. Money is a unique commodity that people tend to acquire without satisfaction.

That is why some call it the oxygen of investment. The importance of this oxygen of investment cannot be overemphasized in effectively managing your investment, success, setbacks, and preparing for your retirement. Since money is the oxygen and current required for effective operation in the investment, success, setbacks, and retirement life, there is a need for you to know the different means of acquiring and carefully applying the appropriate ways in your investments and working and retirement life.

There are indeed several ways of acquiring money in society. In some societies where money is loved more than anything else, you will find people going to any length and doing different types of activities just to acquire money. Some go after money in the legitimate ways, whereas others go to find it in most ridiculous ways. Some make money in ways that are acceptable while others go to any extent to acquire money.

When you acquire money in the right way, such money brings in blessings, and consequently utilizing it exposes you to the blessings of greater yields. However, those who acquire money from the wrong and unacceptable ways acquire the money with curses that bring in suffocation and eventual death of such investments that could affect one's retirement life. It is one thing to acquire money and another to know how to handle it properly.

What then are the different ways of acquiring this essential commodity called money? These ways of acquiring money are not new and not exhaustive but are discussed in this chapter to remind you that the way you go about acquiring money would ultimately determine how effective you will manage your investment, success, setbacks, and retirement. These ways of acquiring money include but are not limited to the following:

1. Stealing or cheating others.

One of the ways people acquire money is through stealing and cheating. Those who steal do this by collecting money and properties from other people without their consent. This ranges from ordinary stealing to outright use of arms to forcing people to surrender their money or properties that are eventually converted to money. This stealing could also be carried out through corrupt practices by people who are entrusted with public responsibilities. They usually take advantage of the responsibilities bestowed on them, either through elective office or organizational employment.

This is the most common way people acquire money in some of the societies today. This means of acquiring money is risky and undermines our values. This could also be short-lived as money acquired in this way does not last. The perpetuators end up either in jail or death because this type of money comes with serious consequences that are always devastating. The risks involved in fraudulent behaviour are getting worse in countries like Nigeria with the strengthening of their anti-corruption agencies, such as the Economic and Financial Commission (EFCC) and the Independent Corrupt Practices and Other Offences Commission (ICPC) in Nigeria, United States' Foreign Corrupt Practices Act (FCPA) and United Kingdom Anti-Bribery Act.

You cannot gain financial independence through this means because you will never live a free life since you will either be always hiding or running from the law and possibly those from whom you stole. The problem with stolen money is the perpetual state of living in fear since you do not know who could be after you from your past victims. This book is not meant for those who engaged in this type of money acquisition. If you acquire money by stealing, there is high probability that you cannot effectively manage and enjoy your retirement with the investment that comes through this means. Please do not engage in stealing.

2. Gambling

Another way people acquire money is through gambling. This means of acquiring money is attractive to those who want to acquire money the cheaper way, by shortcut. They want to get rich at all costs but would prefer to gamble their way into all sorts of easy avenues as hard work, they think, would not give them what they want. These are the lazy and greedy ones in our society. Money generated through this means would not last, as those who get it through this way usually end up poor. These groups of people do not know how to value, cherish, control, and invest their money as they got it the cheaper way. All they know is how to spend, and money spent does not return or bring in profit. Hence, what you find in this group is frustration and failure, which is not good for retirement. This book does not encourage gambling as the money acquired through this means would not last nor bring financial independence that is required for a happy and comfortable life in retirement.

3. Prostitution

This is yet another means of acquiring money that is common to our female folks who believe the only available commodity for them to acquire money is by selling their bodies. These groups of people go to any length to engage in sexual activities in order to acquire money. The end result of this is usually associated with sexually transmitted diseases that consume the life of the participants. It is a risky venture and comes with serious consequences that are not worth the trouble. You may not live to benefit a happy and great retirement life as you may be consumed by this act. It is not the intention of this book to encourage anyone to engage in it while working or in retirement.

4. 419 Crimes and Yahoo Boys

This is another way some people in the society employ in their bid to acquire money. These people use all sorts of deceits through telephones, faxes, and emails to defraud thousands of people. Sadly, some countries have become the byword among nations of the world because of these fraudulent behaviours of these so-called crooks and yahoo boys. This has brought shame and disgrace to some countries where these activities are found. This means of acquiring money is not only fraudulent but dangerous and could lead you to prison. Do not engage in it if you want to have a wonderful work, happy, and comfortable life in retirement.

5. Inheritance

Many people in society got their money through inheritance, where a parent or relation died and left behind a great fortune for the children or loved ones for their use. This is common to those whose relations or parents were able to accumulate wealth during their lifetime, only to depart into the great beyond. This means it is legitimate and has value. However, those who benefit from this opportunity often face the lack of knowledge and ability to handle the money left for them. Inexperience and the inability to value, cherish, control, save, and invest the money often results in untimely suffocation and sudden loss of the entire fortune left. When this happens, you may have to wait for another relation to depart into the great beyond for you to get another inheritance.

For you to have someone who cared and worked hard to accumulate money only to leave it for you means you are fortunate. Even though it is a legitimate way of getting money, it is not a good way of acquiring money and becoming financially free. This book will show you the most effective ways to handle this viable and most important oxygen that ensures your financial survival in your work and retirement life if your money is acquired through this means.

6. Working for It

This is the most common way of acquiring money. Those who work hard to acquire money in this way do this through employment. They acquire their money by working for individuals or organizations for years. This method of acquiring money is both honest and noble. Majority of those who acquire their money through this means and who are honest and hardworking usually end up well. This is because their day job provides them with the foundation required for the creation and accumulation of money for their retirement.

The money acquired through this means comes with a blessing. When properly handled, the required oxygen for effective investment makes these individuals prosper and eventually enjoy a happy and comfortable life in retirement. Your day job is supposed to be the foundation you require to build your future and retirement life. Working hard for your money requires that you treat the reward that comes out of that hard work with care. That also calls for adequate knowledge of the proper ways of handling the money that comes your way without which your effort would end in frustration and failure. This book will show you how to earn, value, cherish, control, save, and invest your hard-earned money effectively for the future and enable you to have a happy and comfortable life in retirement.

7. Financial Investment

Majority of those who acquire their money through this way are those who properly utilize the opportunities available to them wisely. When you put your hard-earned income into uses that bring profit, the end result is additional income. When you put your money in financial investment by saving in the banks and buying shares, the result is more money would come your way. It is a perfect means of acquiring money so long as you have the perfect financial skills or the right advice and a lot of patience. The oxygen of investment you require to excel in this field is money and the knowledge to handle it. This book will expose you to these ways and will be discussed in detail in later chapters.

8. Going into Business

The ultimate way of acquiring money is starting your own business. It is the most effective means of getting money if you do your homework and pick the right business. It is also the gateway to getting financial independence that will take care of your happy and comfortable retirement. A well-run business can generate staggering profits and will outperform any other means of gaining wealth. When you work for yourself, the commitment and the burning desire to succeed will propel you to achieve results that will surprise you as the owner of the business.

If you want to be rich, achieve financial independence, and have a happy and comfortable retirement life, your money should be going into your own business. This method is the best but could be the most difficult. It requires strong commitment and sheer determination, as few out of many businesses that start eventually succeed.

Those who eventually succeed would tell you the efforts they had to put into the business before success was achieved. Many years of hard work and sacrifices have always been responsible for their financial independence. If you must set up your business, make sure you are willing to sacrifice, and be aware of the bigger picture from the beginning. You must imbibe patience and avoid pride when success comes your way. You must, however, be cautious of the type of business you intend to embark upon. Remember your hard-earned money, once lost, may be difficult to recover, and that could affect your retirement.

Fundamental Ways of Handling Money

Even though money is the oxygen required to sustain your investment and, eventually, your retirement, your survival and struggles in life will depend to a greater extent on your ability to understand the principles of handling money and the best way to handle the money that comes into your system. One of such principles is your knowledge and ability to handle money. It is the single most important factor that can contribute to a greater extent to your ability to become financially independent and survive in your retirement. Since money plays an important role in the path of your survival in investment, success, setbacks, and retirement, it becomes imperative for you to know how best to handle it.

For you to effectively succeed in the area of investment and retirement, there is a need to know the way and manner you are required to handle the money that comes your way. Whether yours is hard-earned money or another type of income, there are proper and fundamental ways of handling this scarce and valuable resource that determines to a greater extent your degree of success in your retirement. Right from the time we were employed, we have variously been paid our salaries and other allowances, which we receive and utilize in different ways.

Today, if you should reflect back and calculate the total money you have been paid, you would be surprised to realize the amount you have collected and utilized. Whether you have used the salaries and other allowances you collected rightly or wrongly is history. You must, therefore, continue to seek for better ways of handling the money that now comes to you so that you can maximize its yield. To make maximum use of this vital and scarce resource, it is imperative for you to know the fundamental ways of handling money.

Whenever it comes to the issue of money, different people have different ideas on how to treat money in their households, working places, and the perception they exhibit when it comes to retirement. Money has been responsible for the highest number of divorces in many families. Money has divided nations and intimate friends. Money has also united the best of friends. This thing called money, should we run away from it or stay and send it on duty to work for us? Can money really work for us?

While in school, we were told that money was and is still a medium of exchange, but nobody told us how to put this money into use and expect it to bring more yields or profit. We were told of the qualities of money but were not told how to utilize the medium of exchange for more increase. We were also told that money came to replace the barter system and made it convenient for the exchange of goods and services but not the best ways to handle or utilize this commodity called money.

The way you handle money today determines the way you progress or degenerate in the future and, consequently, your retirement. If you look at the lives of individuals, the rich and the successful in our society today, you find most have the attitude of prudence in the way they handle money.

Most of the rich and the successful people today have the zeal and determination to send their money on duty to work for them at one time or the other. What the rich and the successful do with their money is different from what the poor engage in, in their daily activities. According to Robert Kiyosaki, the rich and the successful have discovered the act of sending money on duty to work for them, while the poor are always working hard for the money but are quick in the act of spending their money.

I have also discovered that the rich and the successful do not hold on to money but are more careful when it comes to the utilization of money than the poor. That is why the rich and the successful continue to be rich while the poor continue to be poor. However, you find that those who are rich and successful today started somewhere along the ladder.

The rich and the successful invest by sending their money on errands to work for them twenty-four hours. The act of sending money on errands is not an easy one. For you to invest and send money to work for you requires a lot of discipline, dedication, and determination. These are the attributes that are common to the rich and the successful in the society. If you want to be rich and successful and have a happy and comfortable life in retirement, you must develop the ability to invest and the discipline that is required to enable you to handle the money you earned as the rich and successful do.

If you have a job, you must develop the discipline of drawing up a budget. A budget would guide you to control and apportion the money according to the different ways that make you realize your ambition of becoming a rich and successful person. How many people know how much they consume in a month for food, telephone calls, clothes, and the like in the family? Do you know your liabilities and the cost of those items that take your earnings without adding value to your present situation? Do you take time to reflect on your expenses, or do you just spend, spend, and spend in anticipation of the income that is yet to come into your system?

Those who accumulate a lot of wealth are people who have self-discipline, courage, and the zeal to set aside part of their income for future use and retirement. They have the ability to plant the seed of success for future harvest. When you know the importance of the seed when planted, eating the seed each time you have the opportunity of having the seed at hand, it becomes a waste to eat the seed instead of planting it for harvest. This is the principle that the rich and the successful and high accumulators of wealth use for their future.

Those who accumulate wealth are those who are willing to take the risk of planting their seeds without seeing the immediate yield but have the ability to differ their gratification of the physical manifestation of the seed they have today. Success and wealth accumulation demands patience. Those who accumulate wealth are people who have long-term planning as their focus and have the patience to wait for the wealth to accumulate. They have the ability to look far ahead in the future to what others cannot see. Oftentimes, they regard life as a platform for planning the path for the future of their lives, families, and conditions that affect all that surround them and, of course, their retirement.

The rich and successful discipline themselves and make sure that whatever income they earn, part of it is saved, accumulated, and properly invested for their future and retirement. We notice that most of the rich people around have a habit of deferring their gratification, hence their ability to reduce their lifestyle below their counterparts that may be earning the same amount to keep part of their earnings for the future. This attribute is lacking in many of us who earn and spend completely on things that do not last or create income but vanish almost immediately to the extent that we go out to borrow to be able to get to another payday.

What, then, are these fundamental ways of handling money? They include the following. This list is, however, not exhaustive.

1. Value the money.
No one can under estimate the role of oxygen in the life of a living organism. When your survival and life is totally dependent on the availability of a limited quantity of oxygen, it calls for careful handling of that scarce quantity. Any leakages could result to suffocation and untimely death. This situation is better understood by the medical professionals who are exposed to these circumstances during the course of their duties in the hospitals. Whenever a patient is solely dependent on oxygen, care in handling the patient is always required from the medical personnel to avoid mistakes and untimely death.

In the financial and, indeed, investment field, the oxygen of investment, which is money, is often carelessly treated, and once that happens, you discover a sudden and untimely demise of such businesses. This is the situation a lot of us find ourselves in. Many of us work hard for our daily earnings, and at the end of the month, we are paid our salaries as a result of the work and services we rendered to the corporation. It is surprising to note that many of us find it difficult to even think and plan the way and manner we utilize this hard-earned income, much less prepare for retirement. We often carelessly allow many leakages in the way we handle our hard-earned money, letting it disappear into thin air. We do not value the money we earn.

As mentioned earlier, it will surprise you to know the total salaries and other allowances you have collected from the organization you are working in from the first day you started work to date. If I may ask, what did you do with the salaries and allowances you were paid all these years? What happened to that car loan, those compassionate loans, and the other loans that you collected? For those of you who collected one loan or the other, have you been handling the money that passes through your hands properly? If you value your hard-earned money very much, you would create quality time to think and plan for the purchases that you make or possibly save some for your retirement. If you don't value the money you earn, how can you control it? You have to value your money to be able to make the efforts to control it.

2. Control the money.
The need to control the only source of survival and block all the leakages that could drain the oxygen of investment is to have absolute control of our system. The moment you allow many leakages in your system, this oxygen called money will gradually and systematically escape, and the eventual result is the suffocation and death of your business. You need to develop controlled habits of spending that will enable you to control the oxygen of investment that is limited and scarce so that it will serve you for a long time and take care of your retirement.

However, in most instances, our purchases are based on what we see in the markets and around us and not based on proper planning. We find it difficult to control our emotions when we are paid and consequently, we do not control our hard earned money. Many times, the things we intend to purchase appear clearly in our imaginations when the money has not arrived, but the moment the money comes, different needs and wants immediately appear. Unfortunately, we end up putting our money in uses that do not bring profit or add value to us.

Always remember to plan and have the list of the items already decided on before collecting your salary and use the list as a guide in all your purchases in the market. When you control the flow of the oxygen that is required for your normal survival, you would discover that the salary, other allowances or returns from your daily business activities are sufficient to enable you to live a normal life and even have some to save for investment and retirement. You cannot save when you do not control all those leakages that deplete your resources without replacement in terms of profit or added value.

For you to control your system, you require self-discipline to look at your current situation and also see the future as the window that would secure and guarantee financial independence. For you to control your system, you need to know your total earnings for the month, total liabilities, and the difference between the two. What are you expecting to enter your system within the month and what do expect to spend during the same period?

Apart from this, there is also need to know your net worth. This is your total asset, or all that you have minus your total liability, or all that you owe. The difference is your net worth. Your total net worth should be in the positive, and not only that, experts have agreed that it should be at least thrice your total monthly salary. If you control properly the oxygen of investment, you would discover that all the leakages in your system would be blocked, and your ability to save becomes easier. If you cannot control your money, how can you save? You have to control your money to be able to save it.

3. Save a percentage of the money.
The need to save the oxygen of investment to ensure survival in our bid to be successful in investment, and our retirement cannot be overemphasized. To avoid eventual suffocation, early death in investment, and retirement, there is a need to take careful steps in handling this scarce commodity called money. This is the area a lot of us find difficult to strive. Most of the time, you find people complaining that the money they earn is not enough. Why is this difficult? A lot of people would say, how much should I be paid wherein I could spend and still have some to save? It is not the quantum of what you receive

that matters, but what really counts is the self-discipline to manage even the little you receive. We need self-discipline to set the target of what we intend to pay ourselves, and we need to discipline ourselves to ensure we implement the decision. That is why someone said, 'Á part of all you earn is for you to keep. If you cannot save a part of all you earn, then, the seed of greatness is not in you'.

The moment we get this scarce commodity, we immediately forget the pain we went through seeking for the oxygen of investment, and consequently, we create several leakages that keep draining and allowing this precious resource to escape into thin air. If you cannot control the leakages in your system, definitely, you will discover that you are likely spending more than you are earning. Because of the leakages and lack of financial control of their systems, oftentimes people in this category keep borrowing to survive.

Many of them find it difficult to save part of the money that comes into their system because most of them do not value the money that they spend their energy working hard to get. But the truth is, as I said earlier, it is not the amount you earn that matters but your ability and the discipline to value, control, and save the little you have that really matters. Your financial success or failure will be determined by your ability to value, cherish, respect, control, and save part of what you have today for the future retirement. If you cannot save your money, how can you invest? You have to save part of your earned money to be able to have the surplus to invest.

4. Invest a percentage of the money.
For you to survive as an investor and really prepare for a happy and comfortable retirement, you need constant supply of the oxygen of investment. This oxygen is scarce, and the source is not permanent. If you are a worker today and are depending on your employer as the source of your investment oxygen, that source will, one day, come to an end. You will, one day, either voluntarily resign or reach your retirement age, or you will be compulsorily retired. Whichever comes first will mean the end of the supply of that vital source of income.

It is not just enough to work and earn salaries or returns from your investment; it is necessary to properly invest early in life to have financial independence that would take care of your retirement. For you to have this financial independence, you have to invest your money wisely in ventures that will bring in good yield. This yield, when reinvested over a long time, can eventually be utilized during retirement when the strength to work is no longer there.

The successful in our society today made it because of their ability to invest their money early in life. They have developed a habit of investing a certain percentage of the money they earn into ventures that bring in additional money into their system. In fact, majority of this group invest their money first and spend the rest, whereas the poor and the middle class spend their money first and invest the rest, as posited by Robert Kiyosaki. Many people depend on one single source of income for the supply of the oxygen of their investment, and consequently, any slight effect on the flow of this oxygen in their system leads to immediate confusion and psychological shock.

This lack of control and diversification of the source of the oxygen has contributed to creating several leakages that make hard-earned income escape into thin air. It thus becomes difficult to account for the way it was used when asked. It is wise to invest a certain percentage of your hard-earned money for the future and your retirement.

This is always difficult, but with self-discipline and determination, one can do it. For you to be able to invest, it is advisable to save part of the money you earned, depending on your capacity for it, sometime before spending. The bottom line in investing money is the returns or profit that will accrue on the investment. Whenever you invest, you are making additional money. It's only when you put money into use that you can make it grow. If you don't understand investment, you will be a less effective entrepreneur. If you cannot invest your money properly into ventures that produce profit, how will you make it multiply?

5. Make the money multiply.

Money is like a seed. The moment a seed is planted, it germinates, grows, matures, and produces fruits for the owner. These fruits will not be produced within a day. It takes time and a lot of effort and energy to get to the point of harvest. The gestation period, from the time of planting to the time of harvest, involves activities that determine, to a greater extent, the yield that is harvested. When you put in the appropriate effort and energy and follow the basic and accepted principles, you will definitely have a bumper harvest. For you to apply the basic and accepted principles, you must have the necessary knowledge that is required for a good performance in that field.

If you know the rules of the game and apply them correctly, victory and success are guaranteed. In the field of investment, it is the same. Making money multiply requires a lot of effort and energy with adequate knowledge of the basic and accepted principles of investment. Being the oxygen of investment, survival will depend to a greater extent on continuing and sustained availability of the oxygen; otherwise, confusion and psychological shocks will occur.

For you to survive in investment, you require enough supply of the oxygen of investment. The quantity required will also depend on your ability to seal off all leakages in your system. Once these leakages are controlled and the game is played according to the rules, the oxygen of investment you require for your survival will naturally flow to sustain the entire system and enable you to have a happy and comfortable life in retirement.

When you invest your money and the profit starts coming, there is the creation of wealth and the increase of the quantity of the initial amount invested. The multiplier effect of money is what makes investment necessary for the guarantee of the financial independence that ensures happy and comfortable retirement. The ability to put money into use with the expectation of profit and additional value is essential for financial independence, your success, and a great retirement life. Effort must therefore be made to continuously utilize the hard-earned money into ventures that will make it grow and multiply. When you cannot make money multiply, you won't have any money to share.

6. Share a percentage of the profit with the less privileged.

There is a natural law of life that is applicable to all and which does not discriminate against anybody. There is a time for everything under the sun. There is a time to plant and a time to reap. Money is like a seed. When you plant it, the seed germinates, grows, and matures. There is also a reaping time for the money planted or invested. The successful in society have realized this principle of sowing into the lives of the less privileged.

When you invest money, the profit so realized is expected to be a blessing to the less privileged in the society. That is why you find successful people like Bill Gates being the biggest givers when it comes to donations and having foundations that are contributing millions of dollars to charity. As they contribute to society's needs, their fortunes also expand and multiply. When you give back to society part of what you get from it, the natural law takes effect on your efforts, and success becomes the result you have in your endeavour. When success comes your way, remember the less privileged in the society, and give back to the society through giving to the needy in our midst. The society will be a better place when we contribute to the development of our society, and when the society progresses, you will definitely have peace of mind to achieve more and, eventually, a peaceful, happy, and comfortable life in retirement.

7. Trust in your God.

The ultimate way of handling your money is to trust in the Lord your God for wisdom to handle and utilize the money and, indeed, everything He has given to you. When you trust in the Lord with all your heart and lean not on your human understanding and in every situation you acknowledge Him, He will not only guide you but He will also crown your efforts with success. You will discover that anything you put your hand to do will prosper. The wisdom you need in to invest your earned income will flow naturally, and great ventures will emerge which will be utilized in your retirement.

That is why the Bible tells us to seek first the kingdom of God and its righteousness and all these things would be added unto us. The principles that are required for fulfilling the desired retirement would be dependent on your trust on your maker who is the author and finisher of your being.

Chapter 6
Investment Matters

Time and money are very important assets. Spend them wisely.

—Robert T. Kiyosaki

Whether you are just starting work, working and about to retire or already retired, you have to be ready to confront the issues of time, money, and investment. As I said earlier, if you are just starting work, you need to start with the end from the beginning. The end is in the future, so you must prepare today if you want a better future. There is also the need to know how to invest wisely the proceeds of your hard work. That is why Robert T. Kiyosaki posited that time and money are very important assets and should be spent wisely. You need to spend your time wisely by focusing on the bigger picture. When you focus on the bigger picture, you will be able to see the end from the beginning. Your retirement is the end that should be prepared for on time. Consequently, the money you earn from that employment has to be spent wisely. Spending your money wisely means investing your money wisely. To invest wisely, you need to be aware of the real meaning of investment. This statement is also relevant to those who are already working and about to retire and those who are already retired.

Apart from that, you have to prepare early for the end that is retirement. It is my desire to let you understand and appreciate the proper meaning of investment and the ways to prepare early for your retirement. For those who have read my fist book, you would have read the concept of investments, success, and failure. However, for the purpose of proper understanding of investment, even though there are several definitions of the term investment, we will use the *New Webster Dictionary* definition. This dictionary defines *investment* as 'the act of putting money into use and expecting it to yield profit, income, or return on the money invested'. Many authors avoid using dictionary definitions due to the dynamic nature of our society. I will, however, use this definition due to some of the salient points contained in it. Let us now critically analyze this definition of investment and see if we can draw up better ways of understanding the term *investment*. There are basically three important things to note in this definition.

1. The act of investing money

From the above definition, one important thing we need to note is the act of putting money into use. Some of us have a natural ability to utilize the money that comes our way, but unfortunately, many of us are not good at handling money. Many people have the habit of keeping their money at home and watching it accumulate, thinking they are investing. They derive pleasure in watching their money accumulate at home in their safes. They keep the money at home and continue to pick at it whenever there is a need to buy something till the last unit is exhausted. But you see, money kept at home and not utilized does not add any value. The money does not grow or increase but reduces in value with every passing day due to inflation, which depletes its value. When you keep your money at home, you are not investing. For investment to take place, you have to act on it by putting your money into ventures that will turn the money round.

Some of you save your money in the banks even though there is profit; there are other better ways of investing your money and getting more profit. The act of putting money into use demands proper knowledge of the different ways of utilizing money that are available. This knowledge is scarce. This is so because while in school, we were only taught that money was a medium of exchange and that it came to replace the barter system, but we were not taught on the act of investing money. We did not have formal classes on the act of investing money. What you find is those who succeed did so through trial and error. Hence, the rate of failure is always greater than the success. We, therefore, need to know that investment involves the act of putting money into use that would multiply it so that we can have higher yields.

2. The expectation of profit from the money invested

Another important aspect of this definition is the expectation of profit at the end of the utilization of money. The money invested is expected to work for you and, in return, bring profit. Whenever you invest or put your money into use, the ultimate aim should be profit or added value. If you invest and there is no profit or added value, it shows that investment is not taking place. When you achieve the desired profit, it shows you are succeeding in your bid to investment. Some invest and succeed while others invest and fail. Consequently, different people invest money into different uses. Some invest their money into marrying many wives, building houses, or buying different types of cars, clothes, foods, studies, etc. Whatever thing you invest your money in, the bottom line should be the expectation of additional yields or returns on the money so invested.

Those of you working for organizations and are paid wages, salaries, and other benefits, let me ask you a question: For several years you have been receiving your salaries and other allowances from the day you joined the organization—where have you been investing your money? Those who own businesses must have been receiving returns or profit since they started that small or big business—where have they been investing their money? Some who have the natural ability of handling their money probably have invested theirs prudently. However, it is disheartening to know that majority of people have not invested their money in ways that bring profit or additional yields. The focus in investment, therefore, should be the end result, which is the expectation of profit. This should be the driving force, motivator, and propeller whenever you are investing. Success becomes easier once the focus is right. However, the moment the wrong focus is followed, success becomes elusive. Hence frustration and failure becomes the order of the day.

3. The availability of money

In addition, availability of money is also another important factor to note from this definition. For investment to take place, money must be available. Without the availability of money, investment cannot take place. Money is the oxygen of investment. God in His infinite wisdom has provided oxygen to every living and nonliving thing.

This oxygen is available to both the poor and the rich free of charge. However, in the field of investment, the oxygen of investment is very scarce, and without it, you would suffocate in your investment bid. Imagine a situation where you are given a limited quantity of oxygen to keep you alive. What would be your attitude towards handling this limited quantity of oxygen to ensure your survival, knowing that a leakage would result in suffocation? Definitely one faced with this situation would take care and value this oxygen to ensure survival. It is the same situation when investing, but most of the time, we do not take care and value this limited and scarce resource called money. All we do is to blow it as soon as it comes in. Money is an important factor for the survival of any type of investment. It is the oxygen that is required to keep you active in investment. That is why it is a very important asset that must be invested wisely to ensure a bright future and a happy and comfortable life in retirement.

Other Aspects of Investment

The need to succeed in whatever you do, especially investment, and to have a happy and comfortable life in retirement cannot be overemphasizes. For you to utilize your money wisely, there is a need to have an abundant knowledge of some very important aspects of the investment concepts. These aspects are often misunderstood and eventually misapplied. When you have a proper understanding of these aspects of investment, you will act and invest your money properly and eventually expect some yields and returns. Take real note of these aspects of investment as they will be useful in your bid to invest your money and become financially independent with a happy and comfortable life in retirement. These aspects of investments include but are not limited to the following:

1. Additional streams of income

Additional or multiple streams of income simply means having income coming into your system from more than one source, and the more the sources of income, the more the total sum of income. Income is defined as the reward you receive as a result of services you render to an individual or organization, usually paid on daily, weekly, or monthly basis, generally known as wages or salaries or rewards from the part ownership of an organization or rental services.

There are three basic types of incomes. Earned income, portfolio income, and passive income. The earned income, as the name implies, is the reward that comes to an individual as a result of his hard efforts while working for an individual or organization. The portfolio income is income received as a result of the efforts of individuals or organization that invest in the financing of an organization through the purchase of the shares of a company. The passive income is as a result of mental effort like writing of books or rental services from the investment of houses, services rendered by individuals and organizations.

Anytime you receive income from more than one source you are currently earning, you have additional or multiple streams of income, as some prefer to call it. Many of us have been depending on a single stream of income over the past years, and consequently, whenever there appears to be any threat to this single source of livelihood or stream of income, life tends to stand still. Why? Because we do not have an alternative that we can fall back on in case of any setback. There is, therefore, the need to look beyond our immediate and single stream of income so that we can avoid the shocks usually associated with the unexpected termination of our single source of income.

How can you achieve this? You should be able to identify that which you intend to do at the end of your service with the organization you are currently working. The moment you identify what you intend to do after your service, you should immediately start practising it on a small scale on a part-time basis. This can be done after close of work, during weekends or holidays, and during your spare time. This is necessary to enable you to create a soft landing ground whenever the unexpected end of your job comes knocking. This book you are reading is a result of using my spare time—mostly weekends, public holidays, and of course, my annual leaves—to write it.

The rich and the successful excel because of their ability to generate multiple sources of income. For those who are fortunate to be working either in the private or public sector, you will agree with me that no matter how hard you work on your job, your annual increment would always be the normal 5–12 percent rise on salaries. If you were to accomplish all your set goals and objectives of daily demands of the family, you would need to improve the sources of your income.

You may have to diversify in order to cope with the demands of your personal and family needs. As a worker, you must work hard for the success of your organization while you endeavour to identify the different ways to increase the sources of your income. Think of the different ways outside your working hours that you can enlarge your income when you retire. The moment you identify what you intend to do after retirement, do not wait until you retire. You have to start practising that on a small scale on your spare time, during vacations or weekends. This must not affect your productivity because your job is required to set the foundation of your multiple sources of income. You must protect your job until your new idea can generate income far above your earned income.

2. Extra cash

This term is also known as excess cash but I prefer to call it extra cash. Extra cash, as the name indicates, can be defined as the unexpected money coming into your system that you could do without because of your existing income. For instance, those working either in private or public sectors, your annual leave grant, thirteenth month, housing grant, and other entitlements constitute your extra cash. How do you treat your extra cash that comes into your systems? Many of us have, in the past, spent this extra cash without proper planning. The essence of this extra cash aspect is to prepare you in the best way of handling the money that comes into your system from time to time.

Whenever you have the opportunity of having extra cash, do not be too quick to spend it. First of all, attach value to this extra cash so that you can control it. Always remember to invest this extra cash into useful ventures that will bring in profit or added value. To achieve this, always write down your goals and what you intend to do with this extra cash. Prepare a plan, take action, and do something every day towards achieving this goal. Once you can invest it, you will be able to turn it around and make more money, and consequently, you set your path to financial independence and success.

This money is extra cash because without this money, you can still survive. Since you have been surviving without this extra money expected, you could wait and think of what to do that could add value to it. What happens with most of us is the moment we realize additional money is coming, what comes to mind is how to change our status and not what to invest this money on. But the rich and the successful use the extra cash, money, or income that comes into their system to invest and, hence, become richer every day. Again, some people would say that the rich and the successful have extra cash that they could spare for a business, and that is why they invest. But I tell you, this depends on you and the determination to invest. It also calls for sacrifice and the desire to be financially sound. I tell you, for these rich and successful people, most of them make a lot of sacrifices before committing the cash into business.

I have discovered that these principles are also applicable to all those who are willing to participate in the act of investment. At every level, we have the opportunity of being exposed to extra cash. This also depends on your perception of what constitutes extra cash. When you concentrate on the problems you intend to solve with money coming into your system, then you stand the chance of misplacing the concept of extra money. That is why the education comes into play. If you have a better understanding of the essence of extra cash, then the tendency of utilizing it to your benefits are high.

3. Assets and liabilities

Another aspect of investment people tend to ignore is the difference between an asset and a liability. The concept of asset and liability in investment is essential for a proper understanding of the secrets of the rich and the successful in our society. The rich and the successful are richer partly due to their understanding and the ability to differentiate between assets and liability. There is a need to have a proper understanding of the difference between asset and liability the way the rich and successful perceive and handle the term in their activities of wealth accumulation.

In school, we were taught that assets include everything we have that has value—like our dresses, houses, properties, and all that we have—while a liability is the act of owing someone. Whenever you borrow something, you are liable. However, I have discovered over the years that for us to fully understand and appreciate what constitutes investment, we must understand Robert Kiyosaki's definition in his book Rich Dad and Poor Dad. He defined it thus: 'An asset is anything that brings money into your pockets while a liability is anything that takes away money from your pocket.' From this definition, it means that most of the things that most of us consider to be assets are, after all, liabilities that continuously drain money from our pockets year in and year out, consciously or unconsciously. Most of us make deliberate efforts to continuously put money into the pockets of other people without the conscious effort of adding value to our existing situations.

What most people do is to get into acquisition and purchases of those items that continue to drain their pockets. If you have the consciousness to look around you what you consider investment and assets, it would surprise you to know how much over the years you have deliberately drained from your pockets and added to others your hard-earned money without adding value on yourself. How many times have you made a conscious effort to ask yourself what value you are adding by that car you are driving? Have you cared to check how much you spend on that car? That 'joint' or nightclub you visit every weekend, have you ever cared to check and calculate how much you spend each time you go out?

Make a deliberate effort to reflect and check on all those things and activities that continuously drain your pockets without adding value to your existing situations. The understanding of the difference between assets and liabilities will assist you to monitor your activities and also make you check each time you go out to spend your hard-earned money, whether you are putting your money into other people's pockets or draining your pockets. There is a need to develop the attitudes of conscious consideration whenever you are about to put your hard-earned money out for services rendered by others.

I have also discovered that in investment, this conscious consideration is evident in the rich and the successful. The rich and the successful in the society are the people who excel in investment because of their vast knowledge of what assets and liabilities are, while the poor, who are ignorant of the basic difference between assets and liabilities, find it difficult to think whenever they are putting out their hard-earned money into use, and hence, success becomes difficult too. The rich and successful in our society use their money to buy assets and continuously expand their assets for years. The end result in most instances is financial independence. Whereas the middle class and the poor spend their money on buying liabilities they think are assets. Such liabilities include more cars, wives, girlfriends, and all things that drain resources rather than add value. In the end, the result is frustration and poverty.

4. Good and bad debts

In our society today, we find people who are perpetually indebted in their working places to the extent that when the month gets to an end and salaries are being paid, these people will be hiding because their creditors will be coming around for their debts. In some instances, some parents, in the bid to run away from their creditors, instruct their wives or children to lie. In some organizations, arrangements are normally made for the wives of some indebted staff to come for part of the salaries of their husbands.

I have discovered that many of us have the habit of being in debt. This has actually made some of us slaves to those we borrowed the money from. In most instances, it is extremely difficult to get out of it. Is debt actually something we should avoid? Is it a bad thing to be in debt? It all depends on the type of debt you are engaged in. One of the secrets of the rich and successful is their ability to utilize good debts. A good debt is a debt that can pay itself and even bring more money into your pocket, while a bad debt is a debt that is incapable of paying itself but will continuously drain the remaining money that is in your system.

The moment you go into bad debt, it becomes virtually impossible to stabilize or think positively. If you are a worker engaged in bad debts, the salary becomes the money already consumed, and consequently, what comes to mind is how to settle all the outstanding debts. Those engaged in bad debt are normally preoccupied with how to pay the debts instead of thinking and planning ahead on how to invest in their future. In most instances, after paying some of the debts from their salary, the remaining balance cannot take such individuals to the end of the month. What you find in most cases is the creation of circles that continue to control the lives of such individuals that go into bad debts. The good debt, on the other hand, always pays the debt and also brings in more money into the system of those who go into good debts. A good debt has the ability to make you rich and successful, as it brings in additional money.

The rich and the successful have, over the years, developed the habit of utilizing good debts that enhance their act of accumulation of wealth. For instance, Alhaji Aliko Dangote is among the richest black men on earth today as a result of the good debt he collected from his uncle some years ago.

During the course of my research, what amazed me was that life is full of challenges and those who confront these challenges excel in whatever they do. In whatever you are doing, there are challenges that come to disrupt what you are doing; if you allow the challenges to overshadow you, then failure becomes imminent. However, the moment you confront such challenges, success becomes prominent. You, therefore, need to prepare for these challenges if you want a happy and comfortable life in retirement.

5. Living below one's earnings
Another aspect of investment is the ability of living below one's earnings by expanding your means. Living below your means should not make you starve yourself or go after inferior standards of living.

It is supposed to make you expand your means by increasing your sources of income through looking for ways to invest your income in assets that will continuously bring money into your pocket. If you want to make it in life, make efforts to spend less than what you earn.

The rich and successful are getting richer every day and throughout history due to their ability to live well below their means. They not only live below their means but they also create their means by making sure that their money works hard for them. They have, over the years, developed astute ways of living. Their styles of life are unique and different from those of us who earn and live above our means. The rich and successful have discovered that life does not mean behaving to please those around them but being true to themselves. What others would say about them does not mean anything to the rich and successful people. The moment you develop the attitudes of living well below your earnings, you create a surplus, and this surplus enables you to plan the way to properly invest in ventures that would eventually change your entire life.

For you to become wealthy, you must put into practice the things the rich and successful do in order to become rich. What has worked out for the rich and successful would also work out for you. It is a natural law. The rich and successful in the society excel in their business because they believe that financial independence is more important than the display of high social status.

Many people work to spend, not to achieve or become financially independent, and consequently, they view life as a series of trade-offs from one level of luxury to the next. These habits make them spend their income instead of investing on assets that build wealth. Building wealth should not be something that changes your lifestyle.

There is also need to always live your normal life even when there is increase in your income. The fundamental rule regarding building wealth is that whatever your income, always live below or spend less than your earnings. If you spend above your earnings, you will be indebted, and investment becomes difficult. However, when you live below or spend below your earnings, you create a surplus, which makes it easier to invest.

Most rich and successful people have the habit of living below or spending below their earnings. This, most of the time, is possible when their spouses are supportive and have the understanding of what financial independence means to the family. If, for instance, you have a spouse that has standard in terms of what she wears, the food she eats, and the places she likes to visit, there is high probability that wealth accumulation will be difficult. There must be understanding when it comes to wealth accumulation. A house divided in its financial orientation is unlikely to accumulate significant wealth. It is difficult to accumulate wealth if you spend time, energy, and money on extremely expensive items that are not asset building in nature.

6. Paying yourself first

Apart from living below one's earnings, the rich and successful also have developed the good habits of paying themselves first before thinking of other things that would consume their resources without adding value to their lives. Your consumption habit is a major determinant of your ability to have a happy and comfortable life in retirement and be rich and successful.

Most people spend first and save and invest what is left over. In reality, if you have the habit of spending first, what happens is that you end up spending all, and nothing is left for investment in assets that will yield high returns that can guarantee a happy and comfortable life in retirement. However, the moment you develop the habit of paying yourself first, you will discover that you can invest and still have your expected expenditure covered.

The truth concerning paying oneself first is when you decide to keep a percentage of your earnings for investment first, the balance will still be utilized for the remaining needs and wants that are normally insatiable. If you decide to face the problems you are facing first instead of paying yourself first, you would end up spending all the money, and most of the time, these problems are still not completely solved, no matter the amount of money you have.

The aspect of paying yourself first simply means setting aside, first and foremost, some part of your earnings for investment every month no matter what and leaving the remaining balance for your other needs. Most rich and successful people adapt 10:20:70. This means paying your 10 per cent tithes, utilizing 20 per cent for investment, and keeping the balance of 70 per cent for the remaining needs of the family. This amount set aside accumulates over time while you are looking for opportunities that could arise. Opportunities do not notify you of their coming. Those who are prepared and have the funds eventually utilize them.

The rich and successful send their money and resources on active duty first, and the remaining balance is utilized for other needs. The end result is, they pay themselves first by sending the money on active service that eventually returns with additional money. This requires self-discipline and determination—to be able to set aside a part of one's earnings consistently for the benefits that are not readily seen.

In addition, they have the ability to make use of other people's money in the form of good debt to enhance their success in life. We must learn and imbibe the act of utilizing other people's money and talent from the rich and successful if we want to get out of the rat race and have a happy and comfortable life in retirement. We must also develop the good habit of paying ourselves first before thinking of those things that will consume our resources without adding value and returning additional resources into our systems.

Types of Investments

The investor is someone who utilizes his present resources today for greater future output. He takes calculated risks and ventures into areas that will give him great yield of the resources he utilizes even when he is not absolutely sure of the result. The resources he basically utilizes are his money and talent. He can also use other people's money, time, and resources. For the investor to succeed in his investment, he has to know how to use his talent, money, and other people's money, time, and talents.

A good investor's duty is to find good opportunities where his money is secured, pays well and receives great benefits, and is free from abuse and corruption. The job of the investor is to find the right profession for his money. He treats his money as his employees. He has to be smart by finding the best profession for his money. When he finds the best profession for his money, his money will take care of him. Just as parents take care of their children, a good investor takes care of how his money and the ways his financial employees are being treated.

Unfortunately, most people usually turn their money to total strangers like the money managers who work for big corporations and have no idea or concern about how these financial employees or workers are being treated. They often let their money be abused, mistreated, and poorly paid. When you hand over your money to total strangers, your money will work for the strangers first before your money works for you. When you treat your money or asset with respect, your money or assets will grow and make your life easier while you are working or in retirement.

Good investors take advantage of opportunities when they present themselves. The ability to use other people's money, time, and talent is one of the ways great investors utilize to become rich. The opportunities available to build assets that keep bringing cash flow are properly and promptly utilized. When you utilize other people's money, time, and talents, it makes you an effective investor and business owner. Why do it yourself when you can hire another person to perform better? Business is a team sport. The person with the best team wins. For you to succeed, you need a smart team with smart people surrounding you. When you surround yourself with smart people, you will succeed. You don't have to be the smartest person in the team.

The culture of saving is the first step to wealth creation. True investment begins with the culture of savings. After cultivating the culture of savings, this will create the opportunity of capital creation that will make available funds that can be invested in ventures that begins to multiply. The funds saved and the opportunity that shows up will enable you to think and invest in ventures that will make you begin to have something to invest or multiply. The culture of savings is necessary to set the foundation of the business. This culture should be done in a smart way. You save while waiting and searching for opportunities that may appear. While you are thinking of that business, continue to save until you capture that business opportunity. Opportunities do not wait for you. You have to wait for opportunities.

Use the money saved to start a business. Start with the ownership of a profitable business. You could start with a part-time business before you quit your job. Invest the cash flow from the business into real estate. A real estate that produces positive cash flow is required to enhance the growth of the business. Invest the excess cash flow from the business into paper assets. A paper asset that produces higher returns than a bank savings account is required for the progress of the business. The combination of the different asset is necessary for the success of the business. The route to business success starts with the culture of savings with the same liquidity.

If you want to be happy, comfortable, and rich at retirement, you have to be financially literate. How can you become financially literate? You become financially literate by opening your eyes, your ears, and your mind to all the information that is around you in order to put your money into the different types of business or investments that are available. The Internet, financial magazines like Forbes, and newspapers such as the Wall Street Journal, Financial Times, and Business Times provide wealth of information on the different business opportunities that can enhance your financial literacy.

The different types of business or investment that we will discuss in this chapter are not exhaustive. There could be other types that are not mentioned here. However, you are free to look outside these ones, but note that the ultimate reason to invest your money is the expectation of additional yields or profit. For you to invest and succeed, you need to know the different options that are available and are capable of yielding you much value. The following are some of the ways people invest their money to get additional yields.

Investing in the Banking Sector

The banking sector is a well-known area where many people invest their hard-earned money with the expectation of profit or additional yields. Some use the banks as a means of collecting their hard-earned income. If you use the bank as a means of collecting your salary, you are the one paying the bank for the services they are rending to you, and you pay commission on turnover on every amount that is processed in your account.

If you invest your money and expect profit and added value, there are two ways you can invest in the bank. These are through the opening of a savings account and the fixed deposit account. By saving your money in the bank, you are making money available to the bank for distribution to other investors who come to the bank for loans and advances. Since the bank uses your money to provide loans and advances on which it charges interest, the bank, in turn, pays you interest for using your money. Though this interest might not be much, it is an investment for those who engage in saving money in the bank.

It is the same principle with the fixed deposit account, except that the fixed deposit account is not subjected to withdrawal during the agreed fixed period, which ranges from thirty days to one year. You are expected to keep your money with the bank until it matures before you can collect it or continue, depending on the interest agreed upon.

Since money is crucially needed to sustain you in your investment, you are expected to handle this critical resource with utmost care by avoiding all the leakages in your system. The best way to block these leakages is to try and save a good percentage of your hard-earned money in a savings account with the bank. However, saving your money in the bank will not make you financially independent. Do not misunderstand me. Saving money is good. In fact, it is important to the process of financial independence. It is not the money saved that is important. It is the self-discipline required to save it. You can't expect your savings to carry you to financial independence. This is because the seemingly high interest paid by the banks ends up eroded by inflation.

There is nothing wrong with saving your money in the banks. However, if your goal is to become financially independent and have a happy and comfortable life in retirement, you must learn to save smart. The money you save is only temporarily in liquid, interest-bearing accounts, waiting for a better place to invest. This smart money is then shifted into a long-range, less-liquid investment that is expected to generate very high returns and profits per year.

When you develop the habit of saving your money in the bank, apart from the interest you collect, the amount you save enables your money to accumulate to the level where you can launch yourself into bigger ventures that will increase your yields. There are other instruments available in the banking sector that can be utilized for investment. We are, however, mentioning these ones because they are the most commonly used.

Investing in the Capital Market

When you are preparing for a happy and comfortable life in retirement, another area you may consider in investing your money and expecting returns and adding value is the stock or capital market. This area, in recent times, has been volatile, and many who did not prepare adequately before entering the market have lost considerably. That notwithstanding, today, a lot of people are still investing in the capital market and are making a lot of money. The capital market creates an enabling environment where shares and other securities are traded. Shares represent ownership of a company. Anytime you buy shares, you become a part owner or shareholder of that company.

Public companies have hundreds, thousands, and even millions of owners. Each owner contributes a little towards the capital of the company. This contribution is represented by shares. Being the owners of a company, the shareholders are entitled to dividends and bonuses and are also entitled to vote at the Annual General Meeting (AGM) of the company.

There are basically two types of shares. These include preference shares and ordinary shares. Preferential shares are the shares that entitle the holder to a fixed dividend, whose payment takes priority over that of ordinary shareholder. Ordinary shareholders are the risk-takers of the business. They share the profits and losses of the business. If the business fails and goes bankrupt or folds up, its assets are liquidated, and the proceeds are used to pay its creditors and suppliers first, and the balance of money left is paid to the preferential shareholders before the ordinary shareholders, who are eventually paid last. If nothing is left, the shareholders go empty-handed and consequently bear the risk of the business.

As a private investor, you cannot buy directly from the stock market; you have to go through a stockbroker. The stockbroker is licensed to trade shares in the floor of the stock exchange. The stockbroker charges you a commission called a brokerage fee that is regulated by the Security and Exchange Commission (SEC). To buy shares, you need to open an account with the stockbroking firm, which provides you with investment advice and may also offer to manage your investment.

When shares are bought or sold on the stock exchange, the transaction needs to be documented and confirmed in a central registry, the change of ownership recorded, money transferred, etc. This process of clearing and settlement used involves a lot of paperwork and takes quite some time.

In Nigeria, for instance, these shares are traded in the stock market under the Nigerian Stock Exchange (NSE), which runs the market. A stock exchange is the body that runs the stock market. It is the government agency that regulates the stock market. Presently, a part of the Nigerian Stock Exchange called the Central Securities Clearing System (CSCS) Limited handles this function effectively using computers.

The CSCS acts as an electronic share registry. A CSCS report is sent to investors who buy shares on the stock exchange, indicating that transaction has been officially registered. It indicates how many shares an investor owns on the stock exchange. A CSCS report is normally ready four working days after the transaction, though it may take a little more time before an investor gets it from the stockbroker. The CSCS report is a very important document that can be used as collateral if you wish to borrow or take a loan from the bank. It also eliminates the risk of loss of share certificate. The market is perfect and good as long as you have the financial skills, the right advice, and of course, patience.

The inherent risk that is associated with investing money in the capital market makes it imperative for current and potential investors to understand the benefits and basic principles that are required for a healthy participation in the capital market. There are three ways investors benefit or make money in the capital market. They make their money through dividends, capital appreciation, and bonus shares.

1. Dividends are normally paid in proportion to the number of shares a shareholder owns in a company. This means the more the number of shares you own, the more you will receive. For instance, when a company declares a dividend of thirty cents, it means that a shareholder who owns ten thousand shares in the company will get three thousand dollars as dividend payment. Dividend payment to shareholders is, however, not compulsory. If the company recorded a loss for that year, it may decide to forgo the payment of dividend to its shareholders.

2. The shareholders also enjoy capital appreciation whenever there is a rise in the price of a share. If you buy a share at five dollars and its price rises to ten dollars, your investment has appreciated by five dollars in value.

3. It is not all the time that companies pay dividends when profit is made. Some companies may decide to reinvest the profit. Whenever this happens, the value of the company increases, and consequently, to reward the shareholders, the company can create new shares to represent this added value and gives these shares as a bonus to the shareholders.

The shareholders may decide to retain these new shares or sell them, thereby converting them to cash. For instance, a company may decide to give its shareholders one new share to every two held on a certain date. That means that the total number of shares a shareholder owns in the company on the specified date will be increased by 50 per cent.

For you to invest your money into the capital market and expect profit, there is a need to have a good knowledge of the operations of the capital market. You need the guidance of a stockbroker who is authorized to buy and sell on the floor of the stock exchange. Even with the stockbroker by your side, you also need to be aware of other critical things that you consider when investing in the capital market to be able to make it in the market.

1. Ability to filter the market

The capital market is made of thousands of stocks that are there waiting for investors to purchase. In this market, both the good and the bad stocks are available for investors to utilize. The prudent investors would normally go into the market fully armed with adequate information concerning the stocks they intend to purchase. They carefully check and filter the market to select from the multitude those shares that will eventually bring additional yields to their investment. However, many of us, on hearing about the capital market for the first time, are excited, and in our eager need to make quick money, all we do is to purchase whatever we see in the market without proper understanding of the viability of the stocks and what it takes to participate in this market.

The good investors would, first and foremost, study the market to identify the viability of all the stocks in the market and the different companies, and compare the stocks and filter the entire market so as to select the best stocks that would yield a good return on their investment. Where they are not certain, they engage the services of professionals to also sieve the market for them before putting their money into use. In selecting the shares in the capital market, there is always the need to study the market. Understand the basic principles of the capital market to avoid putting your money into shares that would consume your hard-earned income.

For you to excel in the capital market, it is critical to understand the filtering process before going into the market. This requires that you develop the attitude of studying financial books and attending seminars on investment. Also engage the services of the experts, those who know the market and are authorized to operate in the market. You must, however, be careful in the selection of these experts. In selecting a stockbroker, you need to know their past and the services they have rendered to other clients. Your success in the capital market would also depend on the type of people you associate with. To succeed in the capital market, there is a need to spend quality time conducting research, filtering the market, updating records, and reading about different companies and the stock in the newspapers and periodicals.

2. Knowledge of when to enter the market

The act of purchasing stocks in the capital market is not enough. You also need to know the right time to get into the market. Just as there is time for everything under the sun, there is time to come into the market and make good purchases. When you have a good understanding and knowledge of the market, it becomes easier for you to detect the right time to put your money into good stocks that would eventually bring good yields on your investment.

To Paul Getty the great investor, the right time to buy is when everyone is selling. This to him is not merely a catchy slogan, but it is the very essence of successful investment. When you know the right time to come into the market and make good purchases, then you would be able to buy the best stocks at the best price. When you buy at the best prices, it gives you an edge over those who do not know the market, and that would increase the yields of your investment. This would eventually lead you to your financial independence, which can guarantee a happy and comfortable life in retirement.

3. Knowledge of when to get out of the market

Just as you need to know when to enter the market, it is also important to know the right time to dispose of your stocks or when to get out of the market. Your ability to know when to sell your stocks will determine your success or failure in the capital market. A proper knowledge of the activities of the market gives you advantage as to when to keep or sell your stocks. Information is the lifeblood of the successful investor.

When you lack proper information, you would be going blindly in the market, and such could lead to fatal mistakes that could lead to failure. For you to succeed and avoid failure in the capital market, there is a need to get closer to the experts and also develop the interest in learning the activities of the capital market. Knowledge is power. When you acquire the skills of investing in the capital market, you would know the right time to exit the market to reduce the chances of failure.

Investing in Real Estate

As you prepare and look forward to a happy and comfortable life in retirement, another area you could consider and where a lot of people prefer to invest and expect high yields and add value is the real estate sector. This area is a viable area, as money invested in this sector could always appreciate in value. You can build houses and buy land for future development if you start on time. There is high probability that your efforts could build up and you could utilize it when you retire. There are three critical things that would make you succeed in real estate.

1. Ability to find the property

In real estate, investment information is important. There are a lot of properties out there that are waiting for investors to buy them. You may not see these properties if you do not have the right information concerning them. The right information would lead you to the best properties in town, and hence, it is important to know where the property you want is located. If you have the information, you would have the right and correct buy that would eventually bring additional yields and profit. The estate business is one of the ventures that brings in a lot of profit due to the appreciation of landed properties. The easiest way to gathering the information that is required is through the different media like the classified advertisements, estate magazines, and friends of the industry.

2. Ability to fund the purchase

It is a good thing to locate the property you desire to purchase. However, knowing the location and identifying the property is not enough. Your ability to source and obtain the funds to purchase the property also counts. You need to prepare and make available the funds for the purchase of the property. Sometimes you can locate the property but the money to purchase it is not available. That makes it difficult to acquire such a property. What you desire depends on the availability of funds. You may also require the services of financial institutions like banks if you have the collaterals or the mortgage institutions where you can obtain a loan facility.

3. Ability to manage the property

The ability to get the funds to purchase the property is okay, but you still require the ability to manage the property in order to succeed in the real estate business. If your property is not properly managed, the tendency of it deteriorating is high. For you to be able to manage your property well, you must check the type of tenants you give your property to. The tenant that is responsible would treat your property as his or her personal property.

Investing in Your Own Business

The greatest avenue and means of investing your money while preparing for a happy and comfortable life in retirement is business ownership. As mentioned, earlier business ownership is one of the ways people make money. In fact, the ultimate way of acquiring money is going into your own business. It is the most effective means of getting money if you do your homework and pick the right business. Doing your homework and picking the right business are the fundamental pillars that determine your success or failure in your bid to financial independence and eventually having a happy and comfortable life in retirement.

If you really want to be financially independent at retirement, you should get involved in one business or the other. Going into business is the gateway to getting financial independence. A well-run business could generate staggering profits and would outperform any other means of gaining wealth. When you work for yourself, the commitment and the burning desire to succeed would propel you to achieve results that would surprise you as the owner of the business.

If you want to be rich, achieve financial independence and have a happy and comfortable life in retirement, start your own business.

The rich and the successful excel in their ways of living because they have realized the importance of business ownership. When you own your business, the income will continue to flow in, and the expansion of such businesses leads to more wealth and more sources of income to you. As Patrick Snow would say, 'The key to wealth is through ownership, not through a salary.'

The rich and successful individuals have discovered this key to wealth building; that is why they are working for their business. Since they are working for their business, they have sufficient time to plan and strategies on the various ways their business can continue to grow. The act of business ownership brings success and continuous excellence to them. Your salary alone cannot make you wealthy but can lay the foundation of your wealth and success in life. Your job is a good thing, but you must realize that it is nothing more than a temporary vehicle to pay your bills and support your family while you are building your dream. There are basically five critical things you must have to be able to excel in your business:

    1. Your knowledge
    In going into business, most people go into it because they have seen others excelling and, as such, conclude that business is an easy venture to start without proper knowledge. Before you embark on any type of business, there is a need for you to know the type of business you are going into and make efforts to acquire proper knowledge. Most businesses fail because of lack of proper knowledge of the running of such businesses.

    Once a business appears to be running and doing fine, you see others going into it without acquiring sufficient knowledge for the business. The next thing is failure. If you desire to start a business, you have to find out what makes the business tick. The moment you understand the basics of the business, your success is certain. You must undertake a feasibility study of the intended business. The projected incomes and expenditures of the business and the potential market that would patronize the products or services to be rendered would have to be known. All these require proper knowledge of the business you are venturing into. When you are well equipped with the fundamentals of the business, it becomes easier to operate such a business.

The business you intend to embark upon should be the area you have interest in. When you have interest in the business, it will be easier for you to find out how things are done. When you know how things are done, you create the success situation. You build the power to accomplish the goals of your business when you educate yourself. This power comes from knowing how to do the things that are required for the growth of your business. Power is the product of understanding the requirements of the industry. The most successful people in life are the ones with the best information. People with power are people who know how to get things done. Knowing how to do something is sometimes virtually the same as having done it. Knowledge will come to you by having your eyes and mind always open.

2. Your workforce

The most critical factor among the factors of production is the human factor, without which the success of a business is bound to have problems. Your success in your business would depend to a greater extent on the type of workforce you engage to work for you. A motivated workforce would always work harder and put their best in the activities of the organization.

A proactive workforce would always look ahead and perform those functions that would move the organization ahead even before instructions are passed onto them. For you to succeed in your business operations and become financially successful, there is a need to select and recruit the best workforce that would move your business ahead. The processes you would use would be operated by the workers you employ.

Your success or failure would normally be determined by the type of workforce that you employ in your corporation. Your ability to select and recruit intelligent and proactive staff is crucial to the effective operation of your organization. You must strive to recruit, train, and retain the best workforce that would move your organization forward. The growth and development of your organization is important, and as a result, the workforce that would ensure this growth and development must be taken care of. Motivating the workforce of an organization should be a priority of the owner of a business that intends to succeed.

3. Your system

For any organization to succeed, the system in place must be effective to ensure sustainability and growth. A system can be defined as a set of procedures or steps that you place into your business to ensure a predictable outcome each time. Drawing from your experience, learning from trial and errors, or using meticulous planning, you can use effective systems to maximize efficiency and minimize waste. The system you would use to guarantee your success would be such that the necessary checks and balances that are required for growth and development are put in place.

Your financial systems should be such that the sustainability of the organization and the inflow and outflow of funds are properly set up. The other systems, like production, administration and distribution, must be made in such a way that the organization would function. The processes, procedures, and steps in the organization have to function well for success to be achieved. The effectiveness of the enterprise would depend to a greater extent on the effective interactions of the component parts of the entire system.

A good system ensures the sustainability of the entire organization, where potential problems are viewed as a common problem that has the ability to affect the end result of the entire organization. The system offers you the unique opportunity to get the freedom you want the business to achieve. With the system thinking, you can make sure that you implement and maximize all the good business ideas you have every time. A good system allows you to pass high value work to others, allowing you to expand your focus and what your business does.

A good system is critical to the success of your business, as it enables you to make complex repetitive activities simple and easy. The system and procedures enable you to put in place and set out what staff have to do, how it's done, and so on, allowing you to ensure consistent quality and performance. With that consistent quality comes great repeat sales and increase in business.

A good system also allows you to have complex tasks performed by less skilled, less experienced workers. It makes your business less reliant on the individual and reliant on the process machineries and procedures. A major benefit of this, and one that makes you money, is that it's easier to attract and train staff because there are more lower-skilled workers than highly skilled ones. The good system reduces the cost of running your business. You will have high-skilled results being produced by lower-cost labour; you will have increased efficiency because people will know what to do and they will do it well.

Essentially, good systems allow your business to operate and function independently of you and become a business that produces profits without your own l perspiration. This makes such a business a cash machine.

4. Your marketing

Another critical factor that one must consider in operating one's business is the marketing aspect of the organization. Your product or services need an effective marketing set-up. Many businesses have failed because of lack of adequate and effective marketing. So also a lot of products have been sent to their early terminal points due to improper marketing.

The success or failure of your products or services would depend to a greater extent on the type of marketing you adopt. You have to decide on the way and manner you intend to sell and distribute your products or services. This calls for proper study of the existing market. Who are your potential competitors? How are they marketing their products and services? What ways are you intending to improve on their present marketing systems? You have to create a niche and come out differently from those already in the industry.

5. Your products

The ultimate desire of any investment is to put money into use that would bring additional yields. This desire also depends on the product or service that is required by the consumers. The success of your investment depends on the satisfaction that you provide through your product or service to the consumer. If you are able to provide a better product or services, the consumers would continue to patronize your products or services. Their continued patronage ensures your survival and, hence, success in your investment. The business owner must strive hard to provide the products that will satisfy the consumers; otherwise, failure will be the end result. Your product or service must be of high quality for it to retain your business.

6. Your customers

Those who patronize and use your products or services are the driving force of your survival in your own business. Your customers are all those people, colleagues, units, departments, organizations, and countries you depend on for your success. Those that also depend on you for their success are your customers. Your customers are the reason you are in business and consequently, efforts must be made to meet and even exceed their requirements and expectations. Your ability to listen to the expectations and requirements of your customers will enable you to plan and provide the best quality products that will keep your customers glued to your goods and services.

Managing Investment

The inability to effectively manage investment has contributed to some individuals finding it difficult to prepare for their retirement while working. I have also seen people who did well during their working life who successfully retired and collected their entitlement, only to lose it due to inability to manage their investment properly.

In managing your investment effectively, whether you are just starting work, working, about to retire, or even retired, there is a need to first and foremost identify the type of investment you are engaged in. Where are the sources of your resources that you utilize to be able to invest? What type of investment are you engaged in? Do you invest in private business or the estate sector? Are you employed, or are you working for yourself? Are you preparing to retire, or are you already retired? Whatever investment you are involved in now, there is a need to be conversant with the basic principles of the field you are dealing with.

The knowledge of these areas will enable you to manage the act of investment prudently. The efforts and resources you are utilizing requires you invest with the understanding that at the end of the day, more yields would be added to the initial outlay, and additional profit or income would be available to justify the efforts and resources put forth. For you to effectively manage your investments, there is a need to be conversant with the following:

1. Basic knowledge of investment

Investment is the act of putting money into use, and expecting profit or added value requires a good understanding of the act of putting money into proper use in order to achieve success. Most people just put their money into uses they do not know or understand. In any field of endeavour, there is always the need to acquire understanding of the operation of such a field to function properly.

The investment field is not an exception. To go into investment when one has little or no intellectual basis for taking investment's decisions could be disastrous. There is a need for necessary basic knowledge in the financial environment whenever decisions regarding investments are considered. Blind investment decisions could cause you a fortune.

There is a need to spend quality time and energy in acquiring the basic necessary financial knowledge in the area of business you are pursuing. You must have the basic background of the business before venturing into the field to avoid disaster. You can acquire this basic investment knowledge in schools, books, seminars, workshops, the Internet, and other sources. It is like the farmer who plants in season and reaps in season. However, before reaping, he has to plough the land, plant the seed, weed the crops, and wait for the crops to grow and harvest the yield from his farm. So it is in every field of endeavour. The period of gestation is a natural course that is also found in the investment arena. The need to always wait for the harvest period has always been a problem with the people.

In every field of endeavour, there are basic requirements in the performance of functions that bring satisfaction in such a field. In the investment environment, there are the successful, those who take risks, and those who run away from risks. You must follow the process before reaping the proceeds.

2. Engaging the services of experts in the field
For you to succeed and effectively manage the investment of your money in profitable ventures, seek professional expert advice. Since they are experts, they render professional advice where you are lacking in any area of your investment. You need these experts to add value on your investments, as they have a deep knowledge of the basic principles of the area of investments you are engaged in. When you engage the services of experts in the field, they offer you professional and intellectual direction on your way to financial independence. Utilizing the best human resources and financial advisors are the two major reasons the successful in the society excel in their businesses and eventually enjoy a happy and comfortable life in retirement.

The experts in the field will provide the necessary guides that you need and desire to excel in your area of endeavour. When the professional is advising you, let it not look strange or blind to you. You need to be in a position to ask questions that will assist that professional when it comes to investment. However, one must also be cautious of the use of professionals, especially when you know nothing in that field of their endeavour.

3. Investing in an area you have great interest in

Investment in the area of your great interest gives you the zeal to take control of your investment. You discover you are happier and the sacrifices come naturally. The difficulties associated with raising funds are no longer issues of discouragement, but the bigger picture of financial independence reigns supreme and brings encouragement. We are at our very best and we are happiest when we are fully engaged in work we enjoy on the journey towards the goal we establish for ourselves. It gives meaning to our time off and comfort to our sleep. It makes everything else in life so wonderful, so worthwhile.

You must engage in activities that you have great interest in that would stimulate your ability to personally develop yourself in the field. For you to personally develop yourself, achieve success, and continue to succeed, you require an area where your interest is all the time. This would enable you to ask questions that will lead you towards the direction of your ultimate goal of making profits or added value. If you want to invest in the capital market, for instance, you must develop a personal interest in the activities of the capital market by constantly reading the capital market reports in the daily papers, Financial Times reports, Business Times reports, and a host of other investment magazines. This will expose you to the basic principles of the capital market.

4. Proper handling of the oxygen of investment

Apart from investing in the area of your interest, you require careful handling of the oxygen of investment, which is money. The moment you misapply this scarce source of survival in investment, the end result is suffocation and eventual death of the business. However, what normally happens with most people who invest is the misapplication of funds and going into investment based on hearsay. You know that money is a game. If you play the game according to the rules, you win; otherwise, failure becomes inevitable. The leakages existing in your system must be identified and blocked; otherwise, the hard-earned money slips away without warning.

When you control the flow of funds into your system, you will be able to manage the portfolios you have. Those unnecessary purchases and unwanted items that attract your attention must be identified and eliminated if you want to effectively manage your investments and eventually enjoy a happy and comfortable life in retirement. All that is required of you is to be aware of the leakages that may affect the quantity of the oxygen available for your survival in your investment.

5. Ability to defer gratification

To manage one's investment effectively, the need to control your immediate desires when it comes to your emotional decisions is crucial. Many people find it difficult to control their immediate desires and, hence, unplanned and uncontrolled purchases affect their ability to think first before taking action. Those who like the physical manifestation of their money would find it difficult to invest since they will not physically see and touch what their money would immediately bring to them whenever they invest in, say, shares of a company.

The physical manifestation of money is an act that a lot of people are engaged that prevents them from parting with their money when it comes to investment. They hold on to their money because they lack the ability to see the future that holds the physical manifestation of things that could make and change their lives. However, the successful believe in delaying the gratification of what their money would bring. In the investment field, the successful excel because of the ability to utilize the basic investment principles available to them.

Those who are able to defer their gratification for the benefit that could arise in the future eventually would find it easy to invest their money into good ventures that may not immediately bring money but could yield benefits and values that could change their lives, which eventually translate into a happy and comfortable life in retirement. The business environment comprises of different types of people and, hence, different types of business owners with different types of approaches to life and business. There are those that appear to be doing well and those that are failing every minute. The business environment is dynamic and always changing. What we see is a combination of different aspects of the activities.

Chapter 7
SUCCESS MATTERS

Once a man has made a commitment to a way of life, he puts the greatest strength in the world behind him. It's something we call heart power. Once a man has made this commitment, nothing can stop him short of success.

—Vince Lombardi

We intend to discuss the concept of success and show you how to effectively manage it while working and preparing for your retirement or even when retired. A lot of research has been made on the concept of success. Different books and articles have been written by prominent writers describing and defining success. The word success means different things to different people, depending on the situation and angle from which one is looking at it. We need to look at the different ways the word success has been viewed and defined to be able to appreciate and understand the concept.

Today, the most common way some people see success in our society is the notion that success is the ability to accumulate wealth. Since accumulated wealth brings recognition, they equate it with success. Other people measure success by the degree of power, influence, and the educational achievement one is able to acquire. Also, some assume that if they only have good health and nothing else, they are successful.

This school of thought believes that health is wealth, and consequently, having good health means they are successful. Public servants or private workers see success as finding a career they enjoy where they can move up and work their way to the top of the organization. To others still, success is reserved for those things they haven't yet attained. That is why when you meet some people, you think they have already made it in life, but they tell you, 'Oh, I'm not a success yet! I'm not going to be successful until . . .' For them, success is reserved for the things they haven't achieved. We can go and on and on.

What then is success? Success is not only about the accumulation of wealth, the people you know, or the level of your educational achievement. Success is also not necessarily determined by power, influence, material possessions, or accomplishments. It is not about those things you have not achieved. Success is much more than that. As John Maxwell, in his book *Your Road Map for Success*, would say, 'Success is a journey and the picture of success isn't the same for any two people but the principles of success are the same.'

Actually, success is a process. There is no finish line; there are milestones. As you achieve one set of goals, you set new ones in an ever-unfolding journey. As you set your investment plans, goals and objectives, the accomplishment of these plans, goals, and objectives enables you to set new ones in order to move ahead. Success is in phases. This process, when consistently followed for a long time with perseverance and patience, normally results in success and eventually leads to a happy and comfortable life in retirement. This is the success that must be protected and effectively managed along the way and at every milestone or phase achieved to avert failure.

Phases of Success

As a worker, being on your own or already retired, the stages of success are found in the process of success. At every stage in life, you discover different challenges that require different approaches and strategies. Getting through these stages can seem frustrating and discouraging if you concentrate strictly on getting to the end. Your ability to endure and persevere along the way determines the end result.

Many give up along the way, not because they are not capable of forging ahead but because of ignorance of the different approaches and strategies necessary for the success at every stage. Those who are conscious of the stages of success are the few who persevere and consequently attain the ultimate goal. Wherever you are on your success journey, there is a need to be conscious of the stages that are inherent in the journey.

1. Discovery phase

Since success is a journey and each milestone achieved calls for new targets and strategies, you need to discover and rediscover your success path and follow it seriously for you to succeed and sustain the success. The ability to discover your success path and follow it from the discovery to attainment phase is what makes you a success.

The journey to anywhere usually begins with deciding where you want to go. That was properly stated by W. L. Hunt: 'The first key to success is to decide exactly what it is that you want in life.' This phase of discovery and exploration on the journey of success requires proper understanding of where you are going. The road map of the destination you are going must be studied and thoroughly understood to avoid taking the wrong route if you are making it for the first time. You also have to discover the landmarks along the way that would lead you to your destination; otherwise, you may take the wrong route.

This phase being a crucial one, care must be taken to discover and explore the right route because once the wrong decision is made, it could lead to frustration and discouragement, and eventually, failure sets in. As you take your investment decisions, which involves that act of putting your resources into use with expectation of greater yield, you must endeavour to discover and explore the necessary approaches and strategies that would enable you to achieve success.

Many investors are naturally endowed with the ability to handle their resources prudently. This makes them feel as though they are responding to some type of calling. To these people, this stage is a short and easy one. These fortunate individuals seem to have been born knowing what they are expected to do along the success path. Whatever they engage in prospers, and with little or no difficulty, they excel in their bid to succeed. However, others find this phase of discovery and exploration to be much longer and more difficult.

Many are weighed down at first with lack of clarity about what type of work they want to do. These people may have to try hard to discover and explore the different approaches and strategies for them to make it. This phase of discovery and exploration cannot be hurried or forced. If you take time to mentally explore to discover the many possibilities open to you, ultimately you will identify what you want to do. In fact, your success commences the moment you begin the process of exploration and discovery.

Why is it that in the midst of hardship and poverty, you find some people succeeding? Why is it that some people start from nothing to become highly successful? Success is attracted by those who discover and properly define their path on the success process. When you develop and explore the right approaches and strategies required on the success path, you find that success is naturally attracted to you.

Success is simply the natural result of continuous and consistent application of some basic laws and principles along the success path in everything you do. Whatever you are doing whether working to improve your condition in the workplace, at home, or the society depends on the magnitude of the application of these basic laws and principles of success along your success path. You have to discover and exploit these basic principles right from this phase in order to achieve success.

The difference between victory, success, and bitter failure lies in the level of your commitment to look out, discover, study, and apply these basic laws and principles of success. For instance, for the farmer to have bumper harvest, the basic laws and principles require that he must clear the land and the soil, have the seeds, and have enough water, sunshine, nourishment and care for his crops. All of these are individually and collectively important to give the farmer a good and a successful harvest. Consequently, it is expected that you, first of all, try and know and discover the basic laws and principles that are required. This will enable you make the most difference to what you are pursuing in life, whether you are into farming, office work, professional sports, academic pursuits, or business enterprises.

These universal laws and principles of success are similar to telephone numbers in that if you dial the right numbers, you get through to the desired person. Even if you are brilliant, well-educated, sincere, determined, and intelligent, if you dial the wrong number, you will not get through. That is why a lot of people or organizations underperform or even go out of business due to wrong application, ignorance, or deliberate violation of these basic laws and principles.

Remember that ignorance of the law is no excuse. Even if you do not know the laws, you are not excused from obedience to them. Even if your violation of these laws and principles are unintentional, you will still pay the full penalty of failure, frustration and under achievement. It is these basic, universal laws and principles that count when it comes to success. The proper understanding, continuous and consistent application of these basic, universal laws to what we are doing detect the success or otherwise of our ventures.

2. Preparation phase

Once you know where you are headed, the next phase involves preparing to undertake the journey. A lot of people attempt to bypass this phase. They jump right into doing what they want to do, with little forethought or preparation. What is common today is that the moment a new idea or business is out and seems to be booming, many jump into it, only to discover they are in the wrong venture. The pure water business in Nigeria is a typical example. You will remember some years back, when the sachet water business came, many people rushed in without preparing or thinking of getting the necessary certification by the National Agency for Food and Drug Administration and Control (NAFDAC).

Research shows, however, that individuals who take six to nine months to prepare themselves for investment make it more than those who jump in unprepared. The preparation one needs to do, of course, varies from person to person. For some, it's a matter of learning—reading about their field or taking marketing courses. For others, it's a matter of money—saving enough to have a financial cushion before leaving the pay cheque behind. For still others, it's a matter of lining up initial business or setting up a team of professionals to support their ventures.

Usually those who don't take steps to properly prepare before going into investment end up paying the price in terms of mistakes and losses. They, however, learn the hard way from past experiences and later take the needed steps. Do not allow this to happen to you. Fortunately, it's never too late to undertake whatever preparation you need, even if you have to start over again after an initial attempt. And even when you must start over, you should consider yourself a success because you are continuing to move toward your goal. In business, success lies in running the race, not in finishing first or even in finishing the first time.

One of the factors responsible for the success of a lot of people is the ability to properly plan before venturing into investment. For you to succeed, there is a need to develop the attitude of properly planning ahead. When you plan ahead, you create the path and direction you intend to follow towards the future.

The direction you are going is determined by the knowledge of where you intend to go, and if you do not know where you are going, the tendency is that you may end up going somewhere else. This was clearly stated by Yogi Berra, 'If you don't know where you are going, you are bound to end up somewhere else.' For you to know where you are going, you must prepare and properly plan the way you intend to go. You need to spend quality time planning the future today.

The act of spending quality time planning the future is imperative to those who intend to succeed. Each time you take quality time properly planning, there is always a need to reflect on the past. When you reflect on the past, you will be able to see your timeline, which contains both the good and bad events or moments that have taken place.

Those ventures, goals, events, activities, or moments you were able to accomplish and those you were not. Your successes and failures would be clearly seen. This act of planning the future gives you the opportunity of checking and appraising your past, areas of your strengths and weaknesses. Efforts would then be made to take necessary steps that would correct the weaknesses and improve on the strengths. Opportunities and threats are also exposed, and the plan is drawn with a view of utilizing the opportunities and preventing the threats moving ahead.

Most people want to be rich but do not care to spend more time and energy preparing and planning on the most prudent ways of investing their hard-earned resources to enhance their chances of realizing their goals. By spending quality time preparing and planning the future, the successful people are able to correct the mistakes of their past to achieve success and a happy and comfortable life in their retirement. You need to go over your life experiences. For you to be able to plan, you need to develop the skills of personal reflection, which involves the act of pondering on life's events with the intention of learning from them. The events of one's life are best sources of real information.

As a matter of principles, develop the act of setting one hour for a day's reflection, a day for one week's reflection, a week for one month's reflection, and a month for one year's reflection. A year's reflection would expose what you have done right and wrong. When you develop the habit of personal reflection, you would see a lot that has contributed to your development and growth or otherwise. This would give you the opportunity to learn from the mistakes of the past and plan on the best ways and directions you would follow in order to succeed. If you refuse to spend quality time planning for your future, you will not be able to reflect on your past, and if you do not reflect on your past, there is a high probability that your future will go the way of the past.

Proper planning enables you to focus on correcting the mistakes of the past and to concentrate on those things that will lead you to achieve success. If you do not properly plan your future, you won't be focused, and if you are not focused, everything becomes a priority. When everything becomes a priority, you live a planless life that has no direction. A planless life cannot lead you to success and a happy and comfortable life in retirement. You must have a plan for you to succeed and have a comfortable life in retirement. The result of proper planning is success. Therefore, create quality time to plan your future, and success will be yours.

This phase also calls for the setting of goals. Goals are simply measurable aims you want to achieve within a stated time. Goals are the individual steps you take to ultimately lead you to your desired dream. Goals are your day-by-day blueprints that provide achievable targets for incremental improvement. You need goals to succeed in life. You need written goals to move ahead successfully in life. They must be goals that you believe in and are willing to pay the price to achieve them. Your goals need to be positive and in present tense. Goals provide you with a daily routine. They show you where to start, and they establish your priorities. They make you organize and create the self-discipline in your life.

Getting yourself to establish your goals is paramount and one of the building blocks in achieving success and a happy and comfortable life in retirement. The act of goal setting is imperative for success in life. Those who succeed are those who know where they are heading to and have set goals that direct their path in the bid to succeed. If you do not have set goals that direct your path, then you are not likely to succeed. No wonder Earl Nightingale wrote, 'People with goals succeed because they know where they are going.' When you know where you are going, you will definitely go in the direction of your destination.

The goals you set determine the extent to which you will succeed or fail in life. Your ability to set your goals would put you in a better position to succeed. Let us say you are trying to climb the corporate ladder in your organization, and you are not too optimistic about your chances because there seem to be too many people competing for too few jobs at the top.

Your dream is that promotion, but wishing is not going to make it happen. What you have to do is to break down the dream into components you can work on individually and make a list of them. After studying the 'dream' position, you determine that what they want is a hardworking person who can manage a team well and improve productivity. Perfecting each characteristic, they then become your goals you can shoot for.

The first thing you do is be curious about your boss. You need to show your boss that you are eager to work hard and pull greater than your share. One way to do this, obviously, is to come to work early. You also begin to seek out more long-term projects to show you can maintain a certain energy level over a sustained period of time. Then you have to show your boss that you are a team player, that you take the time to pitch in for the group, and that you are the kind of person who makes the people around you perform better. The point is that you must establish specific goals and clearly define them.

Goals are not merely vague wishes or hasty New Year's resolutions. They are tangible action items to be written down and followed. When you know your goals, you need to put them into writing. When you have your goals written, they create a path for you to follow. Having goals that are not written is the same thing as not having goals at all.

Goals must be written before they can have an effect on you. The moment your goals are not written, they become imaginations. Once you decide to write your goals, direction is created, and a path that will lead you to success is made. All that is required is the actual follow-up of the implementation of the goals. When you follow your goals strictly and implement them as stated, you are on your path to success. Those who follow their goals succeed at the end. Whereas those who refused discover too late as failure has already taken place. Never keep your goals without implementing them.

3. Commencement phase

Actually, commencement or starting out to invest is usually a crucial moment of decision. This is probably the most exciting and energizing of the phases. You not only have formed your dream and committed yourself to it; you also have taken action and turned it into reality.

Apart from learning from the successful and applying the basic principles, another most common ingredient of success at this phase is intense action orientation. Most successful people are proactive rather than reactive. Whenever successful people hear of a good idea, they act on it immediately after careful discovery and planning on such an idea. Successful people do not delay after careful study and planning because one decisive action or decision to do something different can change their life.

If you must succeed in life and have a happy and comfortable life in retirement, develop the positive habit of taking immediate action after proper and careful investigation, and whenever you identify what you want in life, do not delay, take immediate action, and go after it with all your strength and mind. Knowing exactly what you want in life and taking immediate positive action attracts success to you and enhances your chances of achieving success in the direction you intend to go from where you are. The moment you understand the way ahead of you, immediately act on it; it becomes much easier to focus on your priorities. The end result would definitely be a more organized life that is heading towards success. When you get the first key to success, then success is already guaranteed.

For you to succeed, you have to believe you can be successful. In discussing the impact of belief on success in his book Global Mind Change, Willis Harman had this to say: 'A person's belief system is an organization of beliefs and expectancies that the person expects as true of the world he or she lives in—verbal and nonverbal, implicit and explicit, conscious and unconscious. The belief system does not have to be logically consistent, indeed, it probably never is.' It is impossible to create success without having the ingredient of believing deeply that you are capable of being successful. It is also impossible to live abundantly without believing that you deserve abundance. Every successful person at some point came to believe that one day he or she would be successful.

Your beliefs about success are no doubt deeply ingrained, and you have to be open to changing them before you will ever succeed. Examine your beliefs to see how they have affected your life. What are your beliefs about success? Do not be afraid to analyze your thoughts more closely; you may be surprised at the barriers you have put between yourself and success, once you think about it.

When you realize that you can change even your most deeply held beliefs, you can come to see that not only is it possible for you to become as successful as you would like in all areas of your life but also that it's easy, and much easier than you have ever dreamed possible. In fact, dozens of opportunities appear to you every day. Profitable ideas flash through your mind, that still voice, but you usually let them slip away without pursuing them with concrete action.

It was in this line that Kazuo Inamori, founder and chairman of two of Japan's most successful companies and author of A Passion for Success, stated, 'To succeed, we must have a desire so strong that it reaches and permeates our subconscious minds.' When we have such a strong desire in our mind, it drives us to succeed in the things that we pursue. Lack of faith in one's ability can be a self-imposing limitation. You must develop the positive habit of believing and having faith in your ability for you to succeed in life.

You must know that you are made remarkable and unique, and as such, you can do unique and remarkable things. So accept the fact that you are remarkable and unique, and you will be surprised to see the remarkable things that you can do. Strive on your uniqueness. Bring out your unique human gifts. Once you can bring out all your gifts, you can change anything you want to change.

For you to achieve success, there is a need for you to have determination and total commitment in whatever thing you are engaged in. Having a set of stated goals and plans does not necessarily mean that one is committed to achieving these plans. The commitment comes when you take positive steps and have the determination to starting by taking an action. You must have a great determination and commitment to succeed the moment a positive idea is identified to have a link to your success.

Once a positive idea is identified, there is always a strong commitment and determination by successful people to the ideals set ahead. Nothing is allowed to distract them from their path to achieving success. Vince Lombardi correctly observed, 'Once a man has made a commitment to a way of life, he puts the greatest strength in the world behind him. It's something we call heart power. Once a man has made this commitment, nothing can stop him short of successes.' The level of commitment you make on your way of life detects the level of your success or failure. Once you are committed, determination comes into action and the desire to drive on becomes easier. Nothing can stop you short of success. This commitment, determination, and the great desire to succeed are the common factors responsible for the success of the successful in the society.

4. Survival and Growth Phase
Your ability to persevere in life is one ingredient that you require for your survival and growth. Many successful people have utilized this for their survival and growth on their road to success. One of the most important lessons in life is that success must continually be won and is never permanent. The same is also true with failure. Since the road to success is always under construction, you must not say you have arrived at your destination or plateau in life.

If you have achieved your dreams and success in life, dream bigger dreams and achieve bigger successes. For you to succeed in life, you need perseverance in travelling on this path of success. Because successful people have developed positive habit of commitment, determination, and great desire to succeed, they are able to persevere for as long as their struggle to achieve lasts. There is no such thing as overnight success.

It takes a lot of positive habits of patience and perseverance to get to success point in life. If you insist and persist on those actions that would contribute to your future pursuit of your goals, you would achieve success early enough. The ability to persevere will eventually lead you to success, often at times unexpectedly. This was expressed by Henry David Thoreau who said, 'If one advances confidently in the direction of his dreams, and endeavours to live the life in which he has imagined, he will meet with success unexpected in common hours.' The zeal and determination to succeed would always make you advance confidently in the direction of your dream, and consequently, the achievement of your success in your field of endeavour meets you unexpectedly. Successful people have understood the need to believe in one's dreams and follow the direction of their dream with patience and perseverance; hence they are able to meet with success in common hours.

5. Attainment phase
This is the stage when you finally attain your full dream. This is the stage you attract more of everything your way—more money, more businesses, more friends, more phone calls, more mails, more bills, and of course, more opportunities. This stage can cause drowsiness and may affect your character. To some people, this phase often brings arrogance and pride.

The past is easily forgotten, and many find it difficult to realize exactly what to do with the success achieved. It is often said that any individual, organization, or nation that does not reflect on and correct the mistakes of the past, its future would also go the way of the past. For you to succeed and continue to succeed in life and have a happy and comfortable life in retirement, you need to develop and practice the act of reflecting on the past, remembering where you came from and looking ahead at the bigger picture.

Most people have a strong desire to be successful in every area of their lives—personal, family, and business. But they do not succeed because they are pursuing success on their own. Those who have succeeded have a lot to give out in terms of their experience and the past and the things they have learnt on their way to success. That is why the successful adopt the attitudes of learning from those ahead of them. If you identify and adopt the qualities of successful people, you too would be successful. This phase requires sustained reflection on the past and learning from its mistakes to be able to face the future success with confidence.

Self-discipline is required at this phase as success attracts a lot of things to you. Whenever you see a successful person, man or woman, observe such people; one common quality that most successful people share is the principle of discipline. For you to succeed in life, you need this ingredient of self-discipline in whatever you do. Discipline has been described as the foundation on which success is built because lack of discipline inevitably leads to failure. According to Jim Rohn, 'Discipline is the bridge between goals and accomplishment.' Yet most people do not associate lack of discipline with lack of success. Without discipline, it is difficult to be successful. Yet when it comes to the concept of discipline, most people find it difficult to adopt and practice it.

However, the possession of self-discipline is the key to your dreams and aspirations. If your goal requires that you write ten letters today and you wrote only three, you are behind by seven letters. If you commit yourself to making ten calls today and you made only three calls, you are behind by seven calls today. If you have a financial plan that requires you to save one hundred naira and you saved none, you're behind with one hundred naira today. The danger comes when we look at a day squandered and conclude that no harm has been done. After all, it was just one day. But add up these days to make a year and then add up these years to make a life time and perhaps you can now see how repeating today's small failures can easily turn your life into a major disaster. For you to succeed and continue to succeed, you require discipline to adhere to the goals set and the plan made. Self-discipline is the master key to success because it unlocks the doors to wealth, success, happiness and comfortable in retirement.

Roadblocks to Success

More than anything else, I believe it's our decisions, not the condition of our lives that determine our destiny.

—Anthony Robbins

When you look at the lives of successful people, you begin to wonder why some people are still in poverty while others are succeeding every day. A lot of literature has been written on this. I want us to concentrate and focus on some of the roadblocks to achieving success and, eventually, a happy and comfortable life in retirement.

Many people struggle in life, and yet success eludes their effort largely due to what I call excuses that keep success at bay. Many look at themselves and conclude they can never be successful—why? Because of one circumstance or the other. Consciously or unconsciously, you find some people expressing and believing these excuses each day they are exposed to challenges.

By expressing and believing these excuses, success is kept at bay from these people who may want to succeed. Because of these excuses, they find it difficult to succeed. Unfortunately all these sorts of excuses are our creation and they block our success. But the reality is not the conditions or circumstances that surround us but the decisions we make each day that actually determine our destiny. George Bernard Shaw has this to say on the way we view circumstances: 'People are always blaming their circumstances for what they are. I don't believe in circumstances. The people who get on in this world are the people who get up and look for the circumstances they want and if they can't find them, they create them.' These excuses will always come, but the way and manner we handle the circumstances will eventually determine our success or failure in life. How many of these excuses creep into your thoughts every day? Let us examine these excuses to help us avoid them in our bid to be successful. The good thing is, these excuses have been proven wrong in the lives of many successful people who have succeeded despite the conditions and circumstances they have faced from childhood to their present success position.

1. Everything was much easier in the good old days.

There is a school of thought that believes that the old good days are better than today each time they are faced with challenges. They would recall those good old days when things were easier to come by. They also attribute the difficulties of forging ahead to the difficulties of the present realities. However, the truth is while these negative, short-sighted people are busy concerned with unemployment and downsizing that is going on today, thousands of small businesses start and flourish every day.

Globally, thousands, millions of people are becoming millionaires each year. In fact we have more millionaires today than any time in history. Think of numerous movies being produced, the books being published, and the new opportunities in the science and technology. Think of many parts of the world that hitherto were closed but today are opening to free trade. In fact, becoming successful is not only possible today; it's actually easier than it used to be. The world is now a global village where we can offer new ideas, products, and services wherever we are and technology will take it out to other part of the world within seconds.

2. I am too young.

Another excuse common among people who keep their success at bay is the syndrome of thinking that success is not coming their way because they are too young to succeed. Sometimes, you hear people saying the reason they are not successful is that they are too young. This way of thinking is a fallacy and a mere excuse. When you look at the late Steve Jobs, the founder of Apple computer, he made his first million when he was just twenty-three, his first ten million at twenty-four, and his first one hundred million at twenty-five.

There is an old saying, 'A youth with a single aim in life arrives early at the harvest.' Youthfulness is, more often than not, an asset. Lack of experience can be rewarded with boldness, daring instinct, and originality. History has shown that most successful people started out completely inexperienced and learned as they went along. If you are a youth, always remember youthfulness is an advantage and could lead you to early success and fulfilment. The steam and energy in you should be properly utilized, and you will be surprised of the potentials God has bestowed in you.

Let your youthfulness give you the boldness and daring instinct to venture into areas others older than you may not be willing to dare. Look at Bill Gates, one of the richest men in the world today, started his company that became Microsoft and also the largest computer software manufacturing company in the world at a young age of seventeen while his partner, Paul Allen, was twenty-one. What about Michael Dell, the founder of Dell computers? He was an undergraduate when he started his computer business that has made him one of the richest men in the world at a young age. The Yahoo! you all patronize today was a handiwork of youths under thirty years. The same thing goes for Google, the world's largest Internet search machine. Sergey Brin and Larry Page, who are in their late thirties, founded this engine that can provide you virtually anything you are searching for in the world within seconds.

3. I am too old.

The same thing is common to the majority of our elderly ones who equate their lack of success with their age. You often hear them complain of old age being responsible for their misfortune in life. 'If only I were younger, I would have ventured into this or that.' The moment you allow these thoughts to occupy your mind, you will find the success you are looking for eludes you. This type of thinking keeps success at bay.

The truth is, some people never discover themselves early in life. The discovery comes in their fifties or even sixties. If you fall into this category, never mind or be discouraged. There are those who have made success in their late years. Napoleon Hill's survey of wealthy people showed that many successful men and women don't reach their goals in life until midlife and beyond. The fact is age in success is irrelevant, and you find many people begin a second or third career, some most successful of all late in life. A man like Ray Kroc made his financial mark in his fifties. He struggled as a salesman who discovered a career and opportunity in McDonald's, utilized it, and became a multimillionaire at a ripe age. Also, Colonel Sanders, founder of Kentucky Fried Chicken, made it in business in his sixties.

4. I have no capital.

The other excuse that people usually give when it comes to issues of investment is the inability to raise the capital required for the investment. You find them saying 'I have no capital to start this venture.' When you think you don't have the capital, you will eventually not have it. Many successful people who have made it in life often started with nothing and grew to be great in life.

Whenever you think negatively concerning your ability to raise capital to start that business, you discover it becomes more and more difficult to get a breakthrough. Once you are able to identify the venture and are willing to share this idea with other people who are ready to listen, definitely the capital will come. What I discovered contributes to keeping success at bay from a lot of people is the thought of lack of the capital to start.

5. I am not educated.

Success can also be kept at bay the moment you start giving the excuse that you cannot succeed because you are not educated. Success in life is often linked to educational background of individuals in society, but the truth is, success is not restricted to only the educated. However, most of those who have succeeded in life cut across the spectrum of society, from the uneducated to highly educated people.

Thomas Edison left school before the age of sixteen, and yet he later invented the incandescent bulb that society is benefiting from today. Look at the life of Microsoft's Bill Gates. He was a college dropout and yet he has also succeeded above all his school mates. You see, these people did not allow their lack of initial education to prevent them from moving ahead. Even though many successful people weren't educated in the formal sense, however, they did acquire an in-depth knowledge of the industry in which they made their fortune.

6. I lack an inborn talent.

To succeed, a lot of people feel and believe they must have an inborn talent, and consequently, they attribute their inability to forge ahead in life to lack of that inborn talent. You can hear such people saying, 'It is because I don't have an inborn talent—that is why I have not succeeded in life.' This act is self-defeating and keeps success at bay from those who have this kind of feelings. If you look at the lives of successful people, you discover that most of them did not show any early sign of being destined for fame, fortune, and fulfilment when they were growing up.

Many people talk themselves into believing that they don't have a special talent or what it takes to change their lives. They go to great lengths to justify their lack of success. Again, everyone in the world has some unique talent, some kind of gift that is special to them. All they need is to discover such gifts, develop them, and success will be achieved. As Paul Getty would say 'I most certainly was not a born businessman.' He was not born a businessman, but he developed these special skills along the way, and today, he is one of the most successful businessmen in the world.

7. I don't have the energy it takes.

Another excuse that often keeps success at bay is the belief that one lacks the energy it takes to succeed in life. You find such people expressing the fact that they don't have the energy it takes to succeed in ventures; others had breakthroughs. To succeed in life takes a lot of efforts and energy. Those who have succeeded expended a lot of energy before they reached that status. In fact, an important difference between those who succeed and those who fail is the level of energy expended.

Every action you take requires a minimum amount of energy to accomplish that activity, especially mental or psychic energy. The greater the desire to succeed, the greater the energy that should be utilized to achieve the required result. When there is a great desire to succeed, the distance it takes no longer matters; what really counts is the end result. The bigger picture and the final destination direct the actions that will eventually lead to the desired success. A low vitality inevitably breeds a low motivation. But all it takes is a tiny spark to ignite the resources that lie dormant within us because the potential energy we have is enormous.

Managing Success

Something in human nature causes us to start slacking off at our moment of greatest accomplishment. As you become successful, you will need great deal of sense of balance, humility and commitment.

— H. Ross Perot

Managing success can be a Herculean task and must be carefully handled to be able to succeed and remain successful for a long time. When success is achieved in the lives of individuals, organizations, or countries, there are the tendencies of pride coming into play. It is human nature that causes us to slack off the moment we experience great accomplishments.

As individuals, organizations, and even nations become successful, that tendency of changing attitude becomes obvious, and it takes a great deal of effort to remain calm. Pride can affect the success recorded if it is not checked. The ability to effectively manage success will also determine the extent to which you will continue to succeed in the future. To succeed and continue to succeed, there is need to look at success and try to manage it properly. Success can be intoxicating and could lead to failure if not controlled. The following are some of the ways we can effectively manage success whenever it comes our way.

1. Keep success manageable.

Success of any degree or magnitude acts as a magnet. It attracts virtually more of everything your way. It could attract more money, more business, more phone calls, more mails, more bills, more opportunities, more friends, and even more enemies. So whether success turns out to be all it's cracked up to be will depend to a large extent upon how ready and willing you can effectively manage and handle it.

Success usually comes with a lot of things, most especially when you achieve success on a straight path without many setbacks. Sometimes the spin of success becomes not only exciting and rewarding but also overwhelming and distressing. This is especially true when success comes faster and soars beyond your original expectations. Definitely, preparing and understanding what success can bring to you can help you effectively manage it to enable you to continue to succeed.

When you have very little success coming into your life, managing it becomes relatively easy. This is because the impact and influence of success in your life will also be little, and consequently, you find yourself still being humble and respectful to people around you despite the success achieved. However, when success comes to you without any effort on your part, it becomes very difficult to control the things that come along with success.

The most important thing is not to let in everything that comes with success but let in only those aspects of success that will keep you succeeding. Never think that you must accept everything success brings simply because it has come to you.

For success to be effectively managed, many successful people and organizations consciously decide to limit or even cut back their businesses. Some choose not to expand their markets. Others decide to take only on those clients, customers, projects, and jobs that they enjoy and refer others elsewhere.

In order to effectively manage their success, depending on their market segment, some organizations raise their prices as a way of keeping their businesses manageable. Some reduce theirs to maintain or attract the segment of the society that would ensure their success. Depending on the side you are, you need wisdom to be able to maintain balance in your success journey.

2. Know your success is here to stay

The fear of failure has led many successful individuals and

organizations to actually fail when they had recorded success in their fields. Nothing can ruin the satisfaction of success more quickly than an ever-present lingering fear that the success we have achieved will disappear tomorrow. Unfortunately, what we are afraid of often eventually comes our way.

For you to succeed and continue to succeed, there is a need to know that every day brings a completely new set of events and circumstances that could create whatever success we want. Consequently, the fear of failure in whatever investment or success recoded must be kept aside. Know that every day is a new chance to play the game more intelligently.

Look ahead of your success and plan on the new expectations that may come your way in the days, months, and even years to come. Whenever you look at the future and estimate the rate of achievement coming your way, you then plan and prepare for the achievements ahead of you. Most successful people and organizations continuously engage in improving in the field they are in and adapting the attitudes of facing those things that create fears. The great inspirational writer, Robert G. Allen, once observed, 'Fear melts when you take action towards a goal you really want.' When you do those things that create fear, you discover that fear melt away. Knowing and believing that your success has come to stay motivates you.

3. Adjust your relationship.

Certainly, success brings changes in the way people relate to you. In some ways, these changes make your life simpler. You may discover your calls may be taken more eagerly. Many doors may open more readily. But in other ways, your life may become more complex. Many people who were far from you may begin to get closer. You may experience an influx of people who see you as their opportunity. Friends and family members may become jealous of you or make new demands on you. And you find yourself a target of people who are not pleased with your success. In fact, success comes with a lot of friends and enemies.

The old and new friends will most likely be around you, showing their support.

While there may be those who are jealous or resentful of your success, there are as many others who genuinely enjoy associating with successful people like you. When you succeed, you need to reconsider these relationships. In our African set-up, you will discover distant relations that did not know anything about you coming to make all sorts of claims. The extended family members will definitely come, those from your locality and in most cases, if you are occupying a political position, those from your state and political zone will come your way. Wisdom is required in handling the success that comes your way in relation to your relationships. Your associations will have to change to adjust to your current position in life.

4. Acknowledge and reward yourself.

In most cases, success eludes people who find it difficult to accept they have achieved a milestone during the course of their lifetime. When you do not acknowledge your efforts, who will? There is a need to acknowledge your efforts and try to reward yourself whenever you have a breakthrough. Find some way to demonstrate to yourself just how you value your perseverance, dedication, and willingness to sacrifice for your goals. You have to give yourself a pat on the back whenever you realize you have made or achieved a milestone in life. Buy yourself a medal or gift to mark each milestone you achieve.

When you acknowledge and reward yourself, it builds and enhances self-confidence. For you to sustain your success and manage it effectively, you have to constantly assure yourself that success has no destination.

5. Acknowledge and thank God.

The truth is, whatever your achievement and efforts, they are a result of the provision of the Almighty God, who owns everything including you. All that you have and own belongs to Him. So you need to acknowledge His provision, protection, and provision. There are a lot of things we take for granted. The gift of life, good health, safety, the miracle of eating, and progress are issues in life that only God can guarantee. When you make progress and succeed in life, you need to acknowledge and thank your creator.

Chapter 8
SETBACK MATTERS

There is no doubt in my mind that there are many ways to be a winner, but there is really only one way to be a loser and that is to fail and not look beyond the failure.

—Kyle Rote Jr.

Failure or setback is a concept that most people detest to hear about or embrace and accept as part of life. When it comes to failure, a lot of people find it difficult to celebrate it. Many prefer to identify with success, and this is usually displayed any time a game is played. It could be a football match or an election. You discover the moment the winner is declared, majority of the spectators or supporters will rush out to celebrate the success of the winning team, while the defeated are left alone to mourn their defeat. At times, the individual affected would feel not only dejected but would eventually begin to look at failure as a bad thing or a misfortune.

Many people would begin to count and blame factors and individuals responsible for their setback. At the end of the day, failure is seen as an enemy instead of a friend. Should failure be celebrated or mourned? How do you see, respond, or react to failure in your daily activities? Do you blame others whenever there is failure or a setback? Do you see failure as a friend or an enemy in your daily struggles? The way you respond to and perceive failure would determine to a greater extent your success or failure in life and retirement. In this chapter, we will treat these questions and also look at the ways successful people view or respond to failure each time they are faced with setbacks in their struggles in life. We will also look at the different ways failure can be effectively managed.

What is failure to you as a person? Failure has been described differently by different people to mean different things at different circumstances.

Some see failure as the inability to attain the desired or expected result in the life of an individual, family, organization, or a country. However, I see failure not as the inability to meet expected result but as the inability to persist and try again after the setback has occurred. Failure to achieve set goals after several attempts can be frustrating, but your ability to continue to persist and endure the setback enables you to realize the ample opportunities that exist in that situation.

Every failure comes with hidden opportunities that only the persistent soul could unveil. A setback could be painful, considering the efforts already expended and the pain of starting all over again, but the ability to strive and move ahead despite the setback usually makes the opportunity open. The moment you accept the setback and give up, failure occurs because the opportunity that came with the situation is lost.

What really makes us fail is the lack of courage and zeal to continue in our struggle whenever we experience a setback. When you give up anytime you experience a setback, you accept it to be a failure. That is why failure is considered the hallmark of success. When you take responsibility of your mistake and seek to correct the mistake, you discover a new starting point of a new effort with new sets of ideas that your previous mistake has brought to you. Life is full of mistakes, and we must face the mistakes of life for us to break new grounds, just as when a baby learns to walk, it has to fall down many times to learn the new skill. Dave Anderson expressed this views better when he said, 'Failure is the hallmark of success. It can be the starting point of a new venture, such as when a baby learns to walk it has to fall down a lot to learn the new skill. Failure is also the mark of a success you have worked for. When a pole-vaulter finally misses in competition, it shows how far he has come. That failure becomes the starting point for his next effort, proving that failure is not final.'

Failure has been responsible for the backwardness of many people, families, organizations, and nations. We often give up after several efforts and attempts along the way without thinking of the end reward. Thomas Edison (1847–1931) failed thousands of times while trying in his passion of inventing new things capable of changing the world and consequently in 1879, he produced the first incandescent light bulb. He had this to say concerning failure. 'Unfortunately, many of life's failures are experienced by people who did not realize how close they were to success when they gave up. If I find 10,000 ways something won't work, I haven't failed because every wrong attempt discarded is just one more step forward.'

This man tried several times without giving up the struggle and efforts of discovering the new invention of the incandescent light bulb that has changed the world. Had Edison discontinued his search after several attempts, we would not have gotten the light bulb today. However, with persistence and perseverance, he was able to have a breakthrough, and today we are beneficiaries of his efforts. I read of a miner who gave up the search for the precious stone just a few metres from what he had been struggling to get.

Why Do People Fail?

In trying to find why people fail, I discovered there are several factors that are responsible for the failure of many people in life. You may have to look at these factors and see if you have any of them. As you read, be open-minded and discover your shortcomings; critically analyze these factors and make amends. The more you accept to change, the more the chances of having a happy and comfortable life in retirement.

1. Poor understanding of people

One of the greatest factors that contribute to the failure of most people is the poor understanding of the human skill. Your success or failure in life is, to a greater extent, a function of your effective relationships in your work environment, school, family, and the society in general. Those who have a poor understanding of people around them usually find difficulty in relating with them. When you understand and relate effectively with people around you, it becomes easier to have them support your struggles and endeavours.

In life, there are those who relate to you effectively, whereas there are those you find difficulty to go along with. When you do not understand the people you are working with, how will you work effectively with them? Those who lack this human skill normally end up blaming others and situations for their failure. When you lack that human skill, you find it difficult to succeed. The end result is frustration and discouragement. The tendency is to give up that which you are pursuing.

When you relate effectively with people, the moment there is any setback, those around you can easily render their advice, and because there is that understanding, wise counsel is made to you without hesitation. How do you relate with people around you? Do you accept responsibility of your setbacks, or do you blame situations and people around you? Moving ahead despite setbacks makes you counter the fears and doubts that you face. You can create time to learn the people's skills by reading books, attending seminars, and listening to tapes on relationship management. Development of your ability to relate with people is a prerequisite to overcoming failure and having a happy and comfortable life in retirement.

2. Negative attitudes

Another factor that contributes to people's failure is the negative attitudes that affect the progress of individuals. When you act negatively towards your setback, the tendency is to feel like a victim of the situation and justification of circumstances that ordinarily would not have mattered. Those who have negative attitudes hardly behave positively in most instances. When you behave negatively towards a situation, it becomes more and more difficult. Your attitude can make or ruin you. Negative attitudes contribute to many people's failures. The negative attitudes that breed hatred and anger in the activities that have to do with our progress in life should be avoided to avert failure. How do you react or respond to setbacks in your daily activities? Do you react or respond negatively when faced with challenges that appear insurmountable? For you to have a happy and comfortable life in retirement, you must avoid a negative attitude and imbibe a positive mindset in your dealings.

3. Bad fit

Many people today are in the wrong profession, and consequently, this profession is not theirs. Some have spent their lives struggling to survive in these professions, only to discover they are a bad fit for the job.

You see, no matter how intelligent you may be, when you engage yourself in the wrong profession or investment, failure is certain. Many people spend their entire lives pursuing the wrong profession and end up not satisfied with what they are doing. These types of people eventually become frustrated and full of regrets regarding that profession that had occupied their lives. Have you ever checked that job you are engaged in to see whether you are enjoying it?

Doing the wrong job can be frustrating and oftentimes brings failure to those who are talented in one area but who found themselves engaged in another area that did not bring the satisfaction that was required. What do you do effortlessly and which people tell you that you are very good at? Do you find your job interesting or frustrating? If you are not enjoying your job, there is need to re-examine yourself and the job you are doing or that profession that is taking much of your happiness and time. There should be a paradigm shift with a view to getting a job or profession you really enjoy. To avert failure, you need to avoid a bad fit in terms of the job and profession you are pursuing.

4. Lack of focus

In everything you do and whatever you find yourself doing, the direction you are heading needs to be known, and focus must be made on the end result. The destination of your focus must be clear for you to succeed. What you find around is a situation where many start the day without any focus on the end result. When you don't have a focus, you will discover you are moving without a direction. The power of focus is important and actually affects and determines your success or failure. When you don't have focus, anything that comes your way becomes a priority. Once you lack focus even on your job, productivity will decline, and consequently, failure sets in where the concentration on the job is not there. People who are not focused do not have direction and this has led to the failure of a lot of people and the disintegration of many organizations.

5. Lack of strong commitment

Your commitment to any course of action determines the success or failure of that action. Your success or failure is a function of the degree of your commitment. Lack of commitment has contributed to the failure of a lot of people. Where there is less commitment, you discover excuses and complaints. When the desire is high, the concentration increases, and eventually, commitment becomes a norm. Hence, the zeal to move ahead, no matter the setback, becomes the order of the day. What brings failure is weak commitment to the things we set up to achieve. The moment commitment is weak, productivity reduces and failure becomes inevitable.

6. Unwillingness to change

One of the greatest factors that bring failure is the unwillingness to change. People find it difficult to accept change. The moment you treat change and setbacks as enemies, you open up the route to failure. Flexibility is required if success must be achieved and a happy and comfortable life in retirement enjoyed. Those who are flexible will find that a situation that is strange comes and goes because of their ability to adapt and fit into unexpected circumstances. Most failures come as a result of the unwillingness to change by people. That is why Dr, Michael McGriffy said, 'Blessed are those who are flexible, for they shall not bend out of shape.'

7. Shortcut mindset

Failure also comes to those who have the shortcut mindset. For everything, there is procedure. For the farmer to get his yields, he must plant the crops and wait for the harvest time. For you to have anything good, you must be ready to pay the price. The price of success is usually paid before achieving success. You must wait and be patient before you reap the result of your hard work. For you to enjoy the dividend of your investment, you must wait for the harvest time. For you to enjoy a happy and comfortable life in retirement, you must prepare early for it. Time is a healer, and what you don't know today, with time, you will know tomorrow.

8. Poor information

Information is power. Lack of correct information has led some people astray. You need great information for you to succeed and have a happy and comfortable life in retirement. If you have the wrong information and you are travelling, the chances are that you would end up in the wrong place. You must, therefore, find out the correct information for you to succeed; otherwise, failure would be the outcome of the day. What makes a lot of people to fail has been traced to poor information. For you to look beyond failure, you need the correct information that will guarantee success. There is need to face the facts of the matter and check the necessary things that are required for the success of a venture before venturing into it. If you are to invest in a stock or buy a land, for instance, there is need for proper investigation of the history of the stock and the land before deploying your resources. Fortunately, in our digital age, information is no longer an overtly expensive or scarce commodity. With access to the Internet, you can use various search engines to source for information.

9. Inability to learn from failure

Another reason many people do not succeed in life is their inability to learn enough from their mistakes. The will to make mistakes and learn from them is the secret of success. Your ability to take calculated risks, make mistakes, take corrections, and learn from them makes you succeed in life. The more mistakes you make, the smarter you become through the learning process. The better your skills are, the better your ability to take calculated risks. To succeed, you have to learn the science of making mistakes and learning from the experience. Failing or making mistakes is not fun but necessary for progress in life. The moment you fail, know that you are at the moment of breakthrough. Wait a minute, ask the necessary questions. What is it that made you to fail or make that mistake? What is it that you need to learn and take corrections from the mistake? That is the point where new things and ideas emerge. Each time you learn a new skill, a new person emerges. You are new because you have a new skill and are better able to face a new world.

10. Inability to turn your failures and mistakes into success

To succeed in life, you need to learn how to turn your failures and mistakes into success. You have to be confident in your ability to make mistakes and correct and improve whatever you are doing in life. Making mistakes should not be viewed as something bad but simply as opportunities to learn new ideas and improve the situation. Mistakes should be viewed as stop signs that enable you to know that it is time to stop and think and learn something new so you can take the opportunity and make progress.

You should always view making a mistake as a good opportunity to learn something new. Anytime you make a mistake, stop, think, learn, and correct the mistake and look out for the opportunity that may be showing up in that mistake. Avoid the temptation of apportioning blames to the situation, people around you, and circumstances. Instead, take full responsibility of the mistake and check for the lessons that need to be learnt from the mistakes and the opportunities that may emerge.

When you learn from the mistakes, you expand your capacity. To overcome setbacks, you have to learn the science of making mistakes and learning from the experience. Failing or making mistakes is not fun but necessary for progress in life. To tackle setbacks in life, you need to learn how to turn your failures and mistakes into success. You have to be confident in your ability to make mistakes and correct and improve whatever you are doing in life.

Managing Setbacks

No, there is no failure for the man who realizes his power, who never knows when he is beaten; there is no failure for the determined endeavour; the unconquerable will. There is no failure for the man who gets up every time he falls, who rebounds like a rubber ball, who persists when everyone else gives up, who pushes on when everyone else turns back.

—Orison Swett Marden

In managing failure, the words of Orison Swett Marden keep coming into my mind as he expresses the need to always look beyond setbacks each time we are faced with one. The best way to manage failure is to face failure with courage and determination. In the management of failure, many often think of the various reasons responsible for their setback and conclude that they are not the ones responsible but that circumstances surrounding the setback are. However, failure and the circumstances that bring them are distinct and should be handled and treated separately.

When you concentrate on the circumstances alone, you are likely going to focus your efforts on the wrong issues. Circumstances may exist and, indeed, be responsible, but the main factor should be self-examination. Looking outside the self often brings in failure. The moment you look outside the self, there is the tendency to accept circumstances, and most of the time, these circumstances are outside the individual's control. That is why it is imperative to, first of all, look at the self and take full responsibility for your situation and, subsequently, other circumstances. The following are ways you can effectively manage setbacks.

1. Handling the fear of failure

In our daily lives, we always come across setbacks or misfortunes that can be devastating. In most instances, our responses or reactions to these happenings do determine the way the future encounters would be. Our experiences in the past make us react to issues or happenings around us positively or negatively. When you see someone acting negatively, most likely, that individual has had a bad experience in the past. Even the way we interact with people around us is a function of our past experience with others. Fear, the false evidence appearing real, has contributed to the inability of individuals and organizations to act positively or negatively to circumstances or situations.

The fear of the unknown often leads us to react so hastily without taking time to think before taking a decision. When things do not work out the way we expect, our immediate response is to become fearful and uneasy. We are afraid that we will lose the money invested, waste our efforts, or forfeit our emotional or physical investment in what we have done. If we are not careful, we start thinking of our potential losses rather than focusing on our potential gains.

Fear triggers worry, and we begin to use our power of imagination to create all sorts of negative images that cause us unhappiness and make us unable to perform efficiently. Fear and worry create anger. Instead of constantly moving forward in the direction of our dreams, we begin to react and respond by blaming other people and other situations for our problems and challenges at hand.

When you face failure as a result of something unexpected happening to you, how do you respond? The fact is that it is not what happened to you that matters but how you handle what happens that make the difference. Your reaction or response to the unexpected setback is important. Most successful people encounter setbacks and failures most of the time. Dr. J. Allen Peterson, in his monthly publication 'Better Families' said it well: 'Everyone at one time or another has felt like complete failure. Many have allowed the fear of failure to destroy them. Actually, fear of failure is far more destructive than failure and, in any area of life, fear of failure can defeat you before you get started.' Always remember, failure is an event, never a person, an attitude, or an outcome. It is a stepping stone, teaching you something and adding to your experience.

Failure should be used as a tool or a stepping stone to reposition oneself more intelligently by correcting the mistakes identified to be responsible for such failure. It should be an opportunity to re appraise the situation and take necessary new steps in the new direction. This assertion was rightly stated by Henry Ford who said, 'Failure is only the opportunity to more intelligently begin again.' Whenever you fail in your bid to achieve a set objective, there is always another opportunity to start again. This opportunity, when utilized, gives the chance to improve and more intelligently do better.

2. Handling little failures

Many people see failure as one big event, such as insolvency of an individual, company, or countries. However, failure is not just a big event but it is also a result of a long list of accumulated little failures that happen due to a little lack of self-discipline in our daily activities. As Jim Rohn would put it, 'Failure occurs each time we fail to think today, act today, care, climb, learn, or keep going today.' We must, therefore, understand the concept of failure. We must place failure in its proper perspective. This perspective is the understanding that failure is a learning experience. When we see failure as a learning experience, it gives us the opportunity to learn. The moment we accept failure as a process that gives us the opportunity to learn, it becomes easier to correct the mistakes of the past. Learning from our past mistakes places us in a better position to do things differently.

3. Handling the past setback

The need to check the past setbacks is imperative. When we check our past setbacks, it enables us to see areas of corrections. Our past setbacks should be a guiding path for our future endeavours. Failure becomes a stumbling block against our success when we continue to do the mistakes of the past. We must develop the attitudes of reflecting on the past. The moment we reflect and correct the mistakes of the past, the future will be different from the past.

As individuals, families, organizations, and countries, if we do not develop the habit of reflecting on the past and correcting the mistakes of the past, the future has a high probability of going the way of the past. It is imperative to check the mistakes of the past and learn from them. Remember: past failures are guideposts for future success. As Bill Newman would say, 'Your past cannot change but you can change tomorrow by your actions today.' What you cannot change, you have to accept it and prepare to avoid it in the future.

The future is pregnant with opportunities and possibilities that, if utilized, will change our destinies. We have the days, the months, and the years ahead to make amends of those things we had done wrong in the past. The false impression of the past can lead us to the truth that rests ahead. John Keats has this to say on failure: 'Failure is, in a sense, the high way to success inasmuch as every discovery of what is false leads us to seek earnestly after what is true.' As we learn from the mistakes of the past, our self-confidence develops and grows. As our self-confidence grows, fear of failing or the desire to always play it safe will diminish. It goes without saying that failure or defeat is hard to accept, but each of us has a remarkable ability to bounce back after such a setback. Often we go on to bigger and better things—even to successes beyond our highest hopes.

4. Handling contentment with failure

The other aspect of failure that most of us do is being contented with failure. The moment you become contented with failure, you become a failure. Never be contented with failure. Abraham Lincoln, in his struggles to succeed in life, saw failure and conquered it. As he stated, 'My great concern is not whether you have failed but whether you are contented with your failure.' Being contented with failure is a sure way to continue to fail.

This is a man who had less than three years of formal education in business in 1831. He was defeated for legislature in 1832. He failed again in business in 1833. In 1834, he was elected to legislature. He was defeated for speaker in 1838. He was defeated for Congress in 1843, elected to Congress in 1846, and defeated in 1848. He was defeated for Senate in 1855, also defeated for vice president nomination in 1858, and defeated for Senate in 1858. He became the president of the United States in 1861. His persistent and continuous attempts after each failure eventually made him president. He refused to give up the struggle to achieve his set goals despite the setbacks he encountered.

5. Handling the ability to stand failure

One of the reasons some people never grow through change is that they can't stand failure. Even the best people have a lot more failure than success. The secret is that they do not let the failures upset them. Life is tough, and we all are going to make mistakes. The greatest achievers have failed several times but got up and still achieved their set goals. As Bill Newman would rightly say, 'I do not think I have ever made a small mistake in my life. But that is where you will find success—on the other side of failure.' A very important aspect of successful people is that they all had failures, sometimes many failures, before having a breakthrough.

Most people never achieved success because they gave up after one or two setbacks. Napoleon Hill's classic, *Think and Grow Rich,* recounts the story of a miner who gave up after months of prospecting when he was just three feet from the gold. This man left the struggle when it mattered most. He did not persevere and endure to reach the end of the struggle and, consequently, left his fortune for someone else who got it at a platter of gold. We must continue to struggle and face our setbacks with understanding and believe in our ability to stand failure after failure in our day-to-day efforts.

Chapter 9
THE COMFORT ZONE

You must consciously and deliberately counter the pull of the comfort zone as you move upward and onward towards ever higher levels of accomplishment.

—Brian Tracy

When it comes to the issues of the comfort zone, whether you are about to start work or already working or even retired, the impact of the comfort zone affects you in one way or the other. In fact, the comfort zone syndrome has the tendency of affecting almost all human activities. Since we are creatures of habit and routine, we tend to resist change in whatever form it appears in our way. The moment we create a habit and routine, it becomes hard to change. In life, when you are in the comfort zone, life seems to go on steadily and smoothly as expected. Often people are happy in the comfort zone not because they are enjoying the zone but because they do not know any other way of living apart from that habit and routine they are familiar with.

The comfort zone is that place where many people spend their entire lives. It is where you feel okay not because you like it. It is also the place where people are prepared to sell out their dreams for a comfortable existence. It is where most of the population settle for second best because they have not got the courage to do anything about changing their situation, which is already part of their usual way of life. A lot of people seem to feel safe in the comfort zone to the extent that anything that would take them outside the zone normally makes them uncomfortable. Incidentally, life in the comfort zone feels familiar, comfortable, unfulfilling, and stuck, and those in the comfort zone do not feel they have any choice but to remain where they are.

Relating the comfort zone to retirement, we need to emphasize the gradual and subtle effect it has on the working class. For those who may just be starting their career, beware of the effect of the comfort zone. This is the time you feel you have all the time in the world, and as such, thinking of retirement at the beginning of your career may not appear necessary. You will also feel you are still young and need some time to settle down. Before you know it, years will have passed you by. That is why you need to begin your career with the end from the beginning and be proactive.

For those already working, you will recall your early years when you started that job. A lot of people find it difficult to prepare early for retirement because of the comfort of their offices, incentives granted to them by their organizations, and other benefits they are conversant and comfortable with. Consequently, due to the effect of the comfort zone, these individuals end up with the ritual of continued endurance and working without thinking of preparing for retirement. Before you know it, time is gone and retirement is knocking at the doors.

In the comfort zone are the familiar things, things we enjoy doing. Safety and relaxation are the things that are in the comfort zone. Safety, security, and freedom from risks are the order of the day in the comfort zone. Outside the comfort zone are the unfamiliar, frightening, and new, never-tried ventures. Fear and risks are prerequisites if you want to enjoy a happy and comfortable life in retirement, and incidentally, these are the unfriendly companions of the comfort zone.

The biggest rewards in life are usually found outside the comfort zone. Outside the comfort zone lie the opportunities, the threats, and risks that are required to make progress in life. If you remain in the comfort zone, there will be no progress. You have to find your way out of the comfort zone and overcome your fears for you to make the desired progress in life. If you desire to make progress in life and have a happy and comfortable life in retirement, you must desire to move out of the comfort zone to meet the new opportunities, the threats, and the risks that would guarantee your progress and the joy of a comfortable retirement life.

In order to win, sometimes you have to do things that are uncomfortable, difficult, and even scary. Outside the comfort zone lie new opportunities, threats, and risks that are required to make progress in life. If you remain in the comfort zone, there will be no progress as the new opportunities that are out there will not be utilized. That is why you must make conscious, right choices and deliberate efforts to counter the pull of the comfort zone in your bid to accomplish your goals in life.

The fact is, the effect of the comfort zone appears mostly when you are succeeding in life. People get to certain levels of success in life and get too comfortable. At these levels of success, the need for improvement ceases to be a motivator, and before you know it, setbacks and failures show up. The lack of continuous improvement leads to extinction or obsolescence, which eventually culminates into frustration and anger.

The comfort zone breeds complacency and laziness. Having experienced an extended period of prosperity, health, and wealth, we tend to become complacent and stop doing what we did to get us there. We become like the frog in the boiling water that doesn't jump to his freedom because the warming is so incremental and insidious that he doesn't notice he is getting cooked. We must, therefore, be conscious of the subtle effect of the comfort zone in every area of our lives if we want tohave a happy and comfortable life in retirement.

'No pain, no gain' is a slogan often popularly said. When it comes to success in life, many people are not successful simply because they are not willing to go through the pain that comes with success. To be successful, to have great wealth, good health, and happiness and to enjoy a comfortable retirement life, there is a need to understand the pain or discomfort that exists outside the comfort zone. The popular saying that nothing good comes easy explains the concept of the comfort zone and, of course, good and bad pain or discomfort.

The comfort zone being a familiar territory, if not checked, could subtly influence our attitudes and make it difficult to change or notice the changes that are happening in the environment in which we live. Change is a constant and happening everywhere. Only those who take time to observe the little changes around them will be better placed to handle the major changes that occur all around the environment.

In the comfort zone, you are either too comfortable or too afraid to change or accept change. You may not necessarily be enjoying the situation or the environment. The fear of leaving the comfort zone can prevent you from finding new opportunities. Most of the time, what you are afraid of is never as bad as what you imagine. The fear you have will make you think of what will go wrong instead of what will go right. The comfort zone is full of old beliefs, and old beliefs do not lead you to new opportunities that are outside the comfort zone. There is need for you to search for new beliefs outside the comfort zone in order to make progress in life. New beliefs will enable you to accept new behaviours. When you change your old beliefs, you change what you do and, consequently, meet new opportunities.

To have great wealth, good health, and happiness and have a comfortable retirement life, there is a need to appreciate the difference between good and bad pain. When you are willing to go through good pain in order to avoid the bad pain or discomfort, there is a need to focus on the benefit that will accrue after the pain. Unfortunately, most people avoid doing what they know they should do because of the pain or discomfort, and they end up in more pain or discomfort. For instance, a person knows he/she should go to the gym and exercise but chooses to have a drink and a big dinner and then watch television. Going to the gym would be an example of good pain or discomfort while being sick, unhappy, unhealthy, unattractive, or overweight as a result of drinking, eating, and inactivity is an example of bad pain.

Check yourself and ask yourself, 'Where have I been avoiding good pain or discomfort when I know it will be beneficial to me?' No wonder Martin Luther King Jr. said, 'The ultimate measure of a man is not where he stands at times of comfort or convenience, but where he stands at times of challenge.' When you press on despite difficulties and hardships, that is when you can earn yourself improvement in life. If it is hard, awkward and tedious, so be it. Still go ahead and face that fear, that exercise; endure that initial pain and focus on the benefit of good health.

Many people are not wealthy today because most of them do not want to go through the emotional and physical pain or discomfort that accompanies the process of making wealth. When it comes to making wealth and becoming successful, they are emotionally, mentally, physically, and spiritually not educated and willing to take the pain or discomfort of implementing the secrets of making wealth. You have to pay the price for you to get the right result.

If they were to mentally learn the secrets of wealth creation, their emotional intelligence about wealth creation would hold them back and would not let them be willing to go through the pain or discomfort that will make them wealthy. If you are to increase your financial IQ, you must take care of the fear intelligence that has to do with your mental, emotional, physical, and spiritual state to be able to operate between good and bad, fear and greed, risk and security, known and unknown, stop and go, action and inaction. Between the extremes are where intelligence and the courage to exit the comfort zone are found. You either pay the price now and enjoy in the future or enjoy now and pay the price later. But you will always have to pay the price now if you want the right result.

From the research of this book, I discovered there are many factors responsible for the majority of people spending their entire lives in the comfort zone. This list is not exhaustive as different people have different reasons why the comfort zone is attractive to them. The following are some of the reasons many people continue to stay in the comfort zone:

1. Fear of the unknown

One of the main reasons you find people spending a greater part of their lives in the comfort zone is the fear of the unknown. The False Evidence Appearing Real (FEAR) syndrome has prevented a lot of people from leaving where they are to a place that could be better than where they are. This is due to the belief that the unknown is delicate and may be worse than the known. This false evidence syndrome, if not checked, can prevent innovation and initiative in an individual's, organization's, or country's life. What appears to be real may end up not taking place or occurring at all. This has, to some extent, prevented a lot of innovations and change to take place.

Fear and risks are prerequisites if you want to enjoy a life of success and adventure, and incidentally, these are the unfriendly companions of the comfort zone. The biggest rewards in life are usually found outside the comfort zone. Outside the comfort zone lie the opportunities, the threats, and the risks that are required to make progress in life. If you remain in the comfort zone, there will be no progress. You have to find your way out of the comfort zone and overcome your fears if you desire to meet new opportunities and enjoy a comfortable retirement life.

The fear you allow to build up in your mind is worse than the situation that actually exists. The old thinking in the comfort zone can becloud you with worries and fears. The old thinking in the comfort zone could also lead to focusing you on what could go wrong instead of what could go right. Old beliefs incidentally do not lead to new opportunities. Your new beliefs naturally encourage new behaviours, which eventually lead to new opportunities that are found outside the comfort zone. The effect of the comfort zone breeds fear of what is happening outside. What you are afraid of is never as bad as what you imagine.

2. Resistance to change

A lot of people resist change most of the times partly because of the syndrome of the comfort zone. Once a habit is created, it becomes difficult to change, and hence, the tendency of resisting change becomes a norm. What you find is continuous procrastination and postponement of action that should have contributed to a lot of progress in such a person's, organization's, or country's life. In such situations, you find excuses, the blaming culture, and all sorts of retrogressive tendencies beclouding the perception of such individuals, organizations, or countries to adapt to new methods and avenues of imbibing new initiatives that would influence the acceptance of change.

How do you view change? Do you like change or hate it? Do you feel secure with the job opportunity you have today? Having a job makes you happy and even makes you feel secure, considering how hard it took you to search and find it. Sometimes things change, and they are never the same, most especially when we are in our comfort zone. If you are not conscious and sensitive in your comfort zone, a lot of things will be happening without you knowing. An opportunity comes your way; when you are sensitive and alert, you catch on it, and it passes you without you knowing when you are not conscious and sensitive. The ability to see opportunity and with it often determinesyour progress in life.

A lot of changes are going on around us just as opportunities are; consequently, you need to be sensitive to your environment. If you do not change, you become extinct. To avoid extinction, you must be sensitive to your environment, gather courage to accept change, and look ahead and anticipate change. Prepare for change, and agree to accept change. To confront change, you have to resist fear. Whenever you stop being afraid, you feel good and encouraged. Just as a life fish goes against the water current, you must go against fear and the comfort zone for you to succeed in life.

3. Familiarity

Another factor that contributes to the comfort zone syndrome is familiarity. To be familiar is to get used to an activity or environment. The moment you are familiar with a particular way of doing things, it is usually difficult to change to a different style. This is because moving from the familiar to the unfamiliar normally brings discomfort. In the familiar terrain, it is easy and okay to remain comfortable. You expend less effort to get things done. In the comfort zone are the familiar things, things we enjoy doing; safety and relaxation are the things that are in the comfort zone. Safety, security, and freedom from risks are the order of the day in the comfort zone. Outside the comfort zone are the unfamiliar, frightening and new, never-tried ventures.

You therefore have to focus on the right perspectives in life for you to eventually enjoy your retirement life. Do not dwell on the problems of life; instead focus on the solution of the problem. Concentrate on the possibilities in life and not on the impossibilities. Think of the positive parts of the solution in life and not the negative. When your perspectives are right, confidence and determination will be the order of the day. How do you view your job? Do you view your current job as an opportunity that would be there forever? Is your job an opportunity that makes you comfortable, or are you so comfortable and familiar with your job that you feel it will last forever? Have you become so comfortable and familiar with the success of your job that you don't notice what is happening in the work environment? The more important your job is to you, the more you want to hold on to it.

Movement into a new direction will assist you to find new opportunities. Staying in the comfort zone environment will prevent you from discovering new opportunities that could change your life. The familiar territories could be deceitful and encourage complacency. When you keep thinking of what you could gain instead of what you could lose, that realization could lead you to the opportunities that abound.

The quicker you let go of the comfort zone, the sooner you find new opportunities. It is better to search outside the comfort zone than remain in the familiar territory, which is not challenging.

Effect of the Comfort Zone

When the matters of the comfort zone are discussed, a lot of people are affected, and at the end of the day, time is wasted as plans are not put in place early to avert unpleasant circumstances. The young would normally feel there is more time and preparing early is not required due to the comfort of their job. For those at the peak of their career, the tendency is to feel time is not available to prepare, and consequently, procrastination is the order of the day. To those on their way out, you find them feeling complacent and complaining of lateness to prepare for time has gone. The realization of the effect of the comfort zone would enable you to check its impact on your life and the retirement that lies ahead. It is better to look ahead and prepare than to look behind and regret. The following are some the effects of the comfort zone that are not exhaustive.

1. Inability to think hard.

The first effect of the comfort zone is that it does not allow you to think hard. It makes most people feel the condition they are will continue to be the same, and consequently, any attempt to move them out would amount to feeling uncomfortable and insecure. It drags people back in terms of their ability to change. Human beings are creatures of habit. Once you have that habit, it becomes difficult to change.

When you begin an activity of any kind and you soon become comfortable with it, you will become extremely reluctant to change what you are doing or change the situation you are in, even if you are not particularly satisfied with it. You then become content and complacent. Eventually, you become afraid to change for any reason. This could create a helpless situation where one is unable to take control or to make any real difference in life.

The individual in this mental state then strives for security rather than opportunities and often feels like a victim of circumstances over which he has no control. They keep on with the familiar activities, attitudes, and habits that are part of their lives to the detriment of moving forward. Their ability to think differently is distorted by the familiar and normal way of doing things as they are comfortable at that point in time. That is why you find some people finding it difficult to prepare early for their retirement. You find some employees complaining their work conditions and environment are not conducive, yet they stay despite the fact that there are other opportunities out there.

2. It is the enemy of human potential.

The comfort zone is the greatest enemy of the human potential. The courage to move out of your comfort zone into your discomfort zone can be hard and challenging. When people get into their comfort zone, they strive to stay in that comfort zone without making efforts to realize the impact it has on their potentials. Often their whole lives pass them by while they are furnishing and reinforcing their little rut of medium performance. You need courage to continually move yourself in the direction of your biggest goals and ambition.

You need to be willing to face discomfort in order for you to grow.

Getting out to the unfamiliar becomes a challenge. You need courage to be able to fight the impact of the comfort zone. Only the strong-hearted and well-focused minds eventually break through the impact of the comfort zone. The influence of the comfort zone must be countered in order to move to a new level. Unfortunately, for most people, the most difficult obstacle is how to tackle the comfort zone.

3. It creates all sorts of excuses.

The comfort zone also affects individuals and creates all sorts of excuses to justify the reasons they are in the zone. I have discovered that those in the comfort zone have the penchant of expressing themselves through excuses to justify why they are in that zone. This is because the comfort zone creates excuses that give you reasons you should remain where you are. These excuses keep these people perpetually in the comfort zone. These beliefs are backed by the excuses or reasons that keep them in the comfort zone. These excuses normally keep their victim comfortable in the zone without thinking proactively into the future and other zones.

These excuses range from these common ones like 'I am not good enough to get what I want,' 'I cannot risk giving up a good salary,' 'I cannot retire now because of my family,' 'I will not get enough or another job very easily,' to 'It is too late to change.' The list can go on and on. You have to stop these excuses and blaming others for your situation. The moment you stop the excuses and blaming others, you will discover that a lot depends on you, as no one will do it for you except you. For you to succeed, achieve a different result, and enjoy a comfortable retirement, you must make commitment and develop a plan to change.

The moment you commit and decide to move on despite the comfort you are experiencing, you will discover that you are making progress. The irony is that if you create enough excuses for not getting your result, you would still walk proudly, tapping yourself in the back, thinking you are in the right place.

Unfortunately, blaming others, situations, and given reasons why you are where you are will not solve the problem. Blaming circumstances by claiming you do not have any option to move out of the comfort zone will not help either. When you stop blaming others and feeling sorry for yourself, you will begin thinking about specific actions that you could take to improve your situation. When you begin to set goals and make plans for their accomplishment, you take control of your life and the future. When you begin learning what you need to know to achieve your goals, you feel more confident and competent in other parts of your life as well. Taking steps towards a great retirement life will guarantee you a happy and comfortable retirement.

4. It brings fear.

The comfort zone also brings fear and makes the individual scared of moving out of the familiar zone and into the unknown. In the comfort zone, most people are scared and afraid of moving out of the zone into the unknown or doing something different. They are overtaken by the fear of trying something new that is unknown, which comes from limiting beliefs that they have about themselves and their abilities. They believe in false impressions, typical of people in the comfort zone while time keeps moving.

The impact of the comfort zone on the life of individuals can be viewed in terms of the false impression they keep that drags them back in their bid to keep pace with the familiar environment while time keeps moving. Only those who have the courage to break out of their comfort zone and take calculated risks will have the opportunity to achieve their potentials in life. For you to make progress and succeed in life and have a great retirement life, you must think outside the comfort zone. The comfort zone can be infectious because growth seems to occur incidentally outside the comfort zone. The choice is yours. No one will do it for you, but you have the responsibility to choose. Step out of your comfort zone, and push yourself out in order to make progress in life.

You can remain where you are or push yourself out of it by planning and taking positive actions that can see you to success. You have to get out there and leave the comfort zone today. Comfort is the enemy of achievement. Get uncomfortable and be happy forever. The things we find in the zone of discomfort should be welcomed as a test of life, and without them, life would be a boring sea of sameness. No pain, no gain.

The comfort zone is one of the major mental effect and obstacles to change. This is because it limits your ability to change your thinking, dream big dreams, and set big goals for yourself. Since you are contented and comfortable where you are, it makes you feel afraid of trying something new and convinces you of the possibility of failure and disappointment.

You therefore need to deliberately aim for the discomfort zone. This is where you win. The discomfort zone is a state you will need to pass through to achieve any significant change. We have to move away from our comfort zone to create solutions where none exist.

Way out of the Comfort Zone

Whenever you are faced with the impact of the comfort zone, you must make efforts to resist its effect. Getting out of the comfort zone can be tough and frustrating. You have to be sensitive to the changes taking place around you. The moment things start getting easy and comfortable around you, that is an indication that you need to start thinking of how to get out of that comfort zone. When it is becoming too familiar, realize it is time to look outside that zone. When you find yourself getting bored and find that you no longer have to try, you should immediately know that it is time for you to head to the next level, to get out of the comfort zone and move into something else more challenging. This could be attributed to the habit and beliefs developed over the period of time one has been in that situation. The comfort zone has a way of keeping its captives stuck and confined to the dictates of the environment. The following ways are suggested, and there may be others apart from the ones mentioned here. Feel free to explore more.

1. Challenge self.

Whenever you find yourself in the comfort zone, you need to challenge yourself and get out if you want a different result. If you want a different result, change your strategy, change your negative thoughts to positive, change your habits, change what you daydream about, change your friends, and change your talks. If you keep doing what you have always done, you will definitely keep on getting what you have always gotten.

If you want something different, you have to start doing something different. Get out of that comfort zone and experience the discomfort of the other zone for you to get something different. You have to give up blaming others and situations and complaining about the environment. Moving out of the comfort zone might take efforts, perseverance, and struggle. It might be uncomfortable, difficult, or even confusing. To avoid these uncomfortable feelings and experiences, a lot of people stay put and complain about it. For you to get out of the comfort zone, you need to stop spending time with complainers and get on with creating the life of your dreams. Learn to replace complaining with making requests.

If you want to accomplish anything worthwhile in life, you must get out of your comfort zone and begin with a commitment, a plan, and a big dream or a vision of what is possible for you. You have to rise above your comfort zone and current surroundings, your existing limitations, and challenges. You have to, instead, imagine yourself sometimes in the future—living the kind of life you would like. You have to project forward into the future—five, ten, twenty years from now—and imagine that all your dreams have come true. You must think about what your life would look like if it were ideal. Where would you be? Who would be there with you? What would you be doing? How much would you be earning?

2. Accept change.
Great success requires a continual willingness to move out of one's comfort zone and change the way you do things. The more you move out of the comfort zone, the more willing you will be to take chances, to step out in faith, and to persist longer than anyone else. If you keep doing what you have always done, you would always get what you have always gotten. This is the common language that is real. For you to have a different result, you must accept change. Change the way

you do things. Do it differently, and you will get a different result. The outcome of those who are in the comfort zone will always be the same; why not get out?

They keep the status quo that is a normal thing to them in all their undertakings. It is their unconscious striving to remain consistent with what they have done in the past that holds them back. This inability to break free of the tentacles of the past is the reason most people accomplish far less than they are capable of and remain unfulfilled and dissatisfied for most of their lives in the comfort zone.

Doing something different from what you are accustomed to makes you feel tense and uneasy. You will notice that whenever you think or do something contrary to your current habit, your impulse attempts to pull you back into your comfort zone by making you feel uncomfortable and uneasy. This is normal because anytime you attempt to move from discomfort towards comfort, you tend to move backwards towards what you are comfortable doing and move away from things that are new, discomforting, and challenging.

In the comfort zone, familiarity is the order of the day, and for you to move out of it, you need to develop the attitude of doing something different that will see you outside the comfort zone. Check the route you take to the office and use an alternative one. Be sure you try new things or learn new challenges one step at a time. Initially it could appear difficult, but with several attempts, it will ease out and make your courage grow. It may be frightening at the beginning, but each step taken will make your courage increase.

The pull of the comfort is strong and attractive. Consequently, you must summon courage and determination to get out of the comfort zone in order to get a different result. That is what Brian Tracy the inspirational speaker said: 'You must consciously and deliberately counter the pull of the comfort zone as you move upward and onward towards ever higher levels of accomplishment.'

The future belongs to the risk takers, not the security seekers.

You must be willing to leave the comfort zone to risk failure, risk humiliation, risk personal safety, and risk losing all your money, your precious savings, your job, and even your life to succeed in life. If you are willing to give up the normal life of the comfort zone, then you must be willing to change the normal habits of the comfort zone.

3. Submit to the will of God.

What is the purpose of your existence in life? The purpose of man on this planet earth is to do the will of the one that gave you life and inspiration to think and reason as a human being. The comfort zone and its effect can be easily overcome if you seek the will of God in your life. With God, all things are possible, including whatever activity that is in the comfort zone. Therefore, we need to seek first the kingdom of God and its righteousness, and all these other things will be added unto us.

4. See each risk as an opportunity.

The main reason why your comfort zone is so comfortable is because it is the one place where you know what to expect. In the comfort zone, there are usually zero surprises. Outside the comfort zone there are a lot of surprises and risks. Anytime you take a calculated risk and consider all risks as opportunities, you will be able to utilize each opportunity and move forward. Each time you don't and begin to see what you may call a risk as an opportunity, you might lose out on something valuable. Begin to see what you may consider to be a risk as a chance for positive change.

5. Face your fears head-on.

In the comfort zone, facing your fears is one single thing that you can do in order to improve and make progress in life. Find out the fears that are holding you back, and take a great step by confronting them with courage. Successfully pushing through each challenge, no matter how large or small, squashes more of the fear that comes up in all of us. Knowing what we have overcome in the past gives us the confidence to achieve and even more. That is why it is not advisable to keep your past failures in the present. The danger with keeping past failures in the present is that you generally stop looking for ways to improve.

As Mother Teresa would say, 'If you cannot change the world, challenge the world,' and the end of fear will be certain. In the comfort zone, there is no room for adventure and excitement. Fear is an illusion and is there to strangle your growth and keep you safe. That is why fear is looked at as darkness while knowledge is light. Just as light causes darkness to disappear, knowledge causes fear to disappear. Forget your concern for what people think of you. Do not be concerned about what people think of you. What people think of you is passive and does not change the real you. Think outside the box. The truth is it is not enough to think outside the box; get used to acting outside the box. One of the biggest things that hold a lot of people back is fear of what people will think about them. Over time, you might feel overwhelmed and trapped by boredom and fear.

Conclusion

It's not what men eat, but what they digest that makes them strong, not what we gain, but what we saved that makes us rich, not what we read, but what we remember that makes us learned.

—Francis Bacon

Throughout this book, efforts were made to let you do one thing or the other that would ensure a comfortable life in retirement. In concluding this book, I intend to end with the words of Francis Bacon, who emphasizes the need to know that reading without remembering and putting into practice the things we read will not benefit us. Whether you are just starting work, already working, or retired, you have to remember and put into practice those lessons of life that make meaningful. Avoid those things that will drag you back in order to make great choices in life.

When you were starting that career, you had several opportunities to make different choices regarding your aspiration of the future. With determination and strong focus, you have been able to achieve some of your set vision, mission, objectives, and goals; consequently you are where you today. For that to happen, you must have faced the pain that goes with it, the pain of disappointment. While working, you must have made some of the necessary choices that made you ensure you end that career in a positive note. Your comfortable retirement will be dependent on the practical steps you will continue to take to ensure you enjoy retirement that ends in your favour. You must be willing to pay the price of success. For you to pay the price, you have to take some practical steps.

Whatever the situation you are, whether you are working or retired, the need to prepare early in your endeavour cannot be overemphasized. As mentioned earlier, just as death is inevitable in life, retirement is unavoidable. In life, all human beings, working or retired, are susceptible to an end in whatever they are engaged in. The issues of life affect all, and consequently, there is a need to imbibe the principles outlined in this book. The truth is, everything I have presented in this book will amount to nothing if you do not have the discipline, determination, and courage to put these principles into practice. Your decision to change and take immediate and positive action towards your retirement will determine your success in life and how successful your retirement will be.

If you have read this book from the first chapter to this point, it means that you are determined, serious, and willing to put into practice the principles in this book and have a comfortable life in retirement. I have actually succeeded in presenting to you what I have read, discovered, and experienced in the course of researching for this book. As Francis Baron said, 'It is not what you read but what you remember and put into practice that makes you a learned man or woman.' Success is a continuous process and full of milestones. Each milestone marks the beginning of another, and reading through the topics shows the determination and zeal you have to have a successful retirement life.

However, it is not only reading through the entire book that really matters; the next milestone is to remember and put into practice the principles of this book. Yes, you have read about preparing early for retirement, the issues of life, which include the concept of investment, success, setbacks, and the comfort zone. Can you recall and remember what you have gained in this book? It is not enough to read this book, but what is important is remembering and putting the principles in this book into practice.

It's not going to be easy to change, but as they say, a journey of a thousand miles begins with a step. The future is brighter for those who are determined to succeed. Dream, think, and concentrate on those positive goals you have set for yourself. Those who have succeeded were able to succeed due to their hard work, passion, and the love they had for the things they were engaged in. You can succeed if you believe you can.

Above all, and as I said earlier, the future belongs to those who are willing to take calculated risks and are willing to rely on the will of God in the pursuit of the kingdom and its righteousness, and all these other things will be added unto them.

About the Author

Mr Zachariah Dauke Suleiman is a holder of a BSc in business administration from Ahmadu Bello University, Zaria, and has an MBA in general management from University of Science and Technology, Port Harcourt, Nigeria. He has over twenty-nine years working experience in the oil and gas industry.

He is an emerging leader and team builder in the oil and gas industry in Nigeria who has actively been involved in adding value to the Nigerian National Petroleum Corporation (NNPC) in its bid to become a world-class oil and gas company. He possesses considerable experience in investment, Nigerian content implementation compliance, leadership, project management, change management, and supply chain management. He was seconded to the Brass LNG project by NNPC as the Nigerian content manager and currently, Manager Efficiency, Corporate Headquarters, Nigerian National Petroleum Corporation, Abuja, Nigeria.

A writer with a strong passion for investment who has authored a book, Investment Success: Your Practical Guide for Managing Investment, he is a motivational speaker and enjoys mentoring and coaching on leadership qualities and investment techniques. He is a Fellow of the Institute of Management Specialist, UK and Fellow, Nigerian Institute of Management.

He hails from Zonkwa, Zango Kataf, a local government area of Kaduna state, Nigeria. He is happily married to his heartthrob, Mrs Martina Zachariah, Esq. The marriage is blessed with two sets of twins, Abrak, Kyangchat, Kazayet, and Kazachat.

He can be contacted at 08036666253 and zdsuleiman@outlook.com.

References

Adelaja, Sunday (2009). *Money Won't Make You Rich: God's Principle for True Wealth, Prosperity and Success.* Charisma House.

Akindipe, F. A. (2002). *Techniques of Making Money in Shares.* Flarmak & Company.

Allen, Marc (1995). *Visionary Business: An Entrepreneur's Guide to Success.* New World Library.

Allen, Robert G. (2004). *Multiple Streams of Income.* John Willey & Sons.

—— (1983). *Creating Wealth.* Smith & Schuter.

Anderson, Nancy (1995). *Work with Passion: How to Do What You Love for a Living. New* World Library.

Canfield, J., Hansen, M. V., and Hewitt, L. (2000). *The Power of Focus.* Health Communication, Inc.

Carlyle, Marie-Claire (2010). *How to Become a Money Magnet.* International Padstow Cornwell.

Carswell, Richard (2008). *The Ultimate Selling Secret: Essential Strategies for Mastering the Art of Business Influence.* Evangel Publication.

Chopra, Deepak (1994). *The Seven Spiritual Laws of Success.* Amber Allen Publishing and New World Library.

Covey, Stephen R. (1990). *The Seven Habits of Highly Effective People: Powerful Lessons in Personal Change.* Simon and Schuster.

Edwards, Sarah and Edwards, Paul (1996). *Secrets of Self Employment: Surviving and Thriving on the Ups and Downs of Being Your Own Boss.*

Pengium Putman Inc.

Fisher, Mark and Allen, Marc (1997). *How to Think Like a Millionaire.* New World Library.

George, Praise (2005). '*Mastering Money: Mastering the Secrets of Financial Freedom*'. Success World.

—— (2005). '*Start with What You Have Where You Are: How to Start and Win Ideas and Dreams*'. Success World.

Getty, P. J. (1965). *How to Be Rich: From Investment to Achievement, Secret of the Millionaire.* Living World Publishing.

Hagee, John (2009). *Life's Challenges, Your Opportunities.* Charisma House.

Hagland, Carol (2011). *Happy Retirement: Simple Ways to Transform Your Relationship, Self Esteem and Emotional Well-Being.* One World Publications.

Hills, Napoleon (1983). *Think and Grow Rich.* Ballante Books.

Inamori, Kazuo (1995). *A Passion for Success: Practical Inspiration, and Spiritual Insight from Japan's Leading Entrepreneur.* McGraw-Hill, Inc.

Kiyosaki, Robert T. (2008). '*Increase Your Financial IQ: Get Smarter with Your Money*'. Business Plus.

—— (2011). *Unfair Advantage: The Power of Financial Education: What Schools Will Never Teach You about Money.* Plata Publishing LLC.

Kiyosaki, Robert T. and Lechter, Sharon L. (2005). B*efore You Quit Your Job: 10 Real Life Lessons Every Entrepreneur Should Know about Building Multimillion Dollar Business.* Warner Books, Inc.

—— (2001). *The Business School for Those Who Like Helping Others,*

2nd edn. Momemtum Media.

—— (2002). *Retire Young Retire Rich: How to Get Rich Quickly and Stay Rich Forever.* Warner Books, Inc.

—— (1998). *Rich Dad Poor Dad.* Warner Books.

Maxwell, John C. (2000). *Falling Forward: Turning Mistakes into Stepping Stones for Success.* Thomas Nelson Inc.

—— (2002). *Your Road Map to Success: You Can Get There from Here.* Thomas Nelson Publishers.

Mbah, Aniekan (2012). *Overcoming Challenges in Retirement.*

McCormack, Mark (1986). *What They Don't Teach You at Harvard Business School.* Bantam.

Newman, Bill (1995). *How to Avoid Detours on the Road to Success.*

Odebunmi, Akin (2006). *Retirement Preparation: A Unique Way to Reduce Stress and Pursue a Healthy Lifestyle.* Atabunmi Nigeria Limited.

Oveng, Paul A. (2010). *Tricks of the Rich: How to Make, Grow and Save Money.* Pearson Educations Limited.

Peeling, Nic (2010). *Brilliant Retirement: Your Practical Guide to Happy, Healthy, Financially Sound Retirement.* Pearson Education Limited.

Peters, Thomas and Waterman, Robert (1993). *In Search of Excellence.* Warner Books.

Senge, Peter M. (1990). *The Fifth Discipline: The Art and Practice of the Learning Organization.* Doubleday.

Sher, Brian (2000). *What the Rich Know & Desperately Want To Keep Secret.* Self Improvement Publishers.

Singer, Blair (2004). *The ABC's of Building a Business Team That Wins: The Invisible Code of Honour That Takes Ordinary People and Turns Them into a Championship Team.* Warner Books.

Sovocool, Erika Welz (2005). *Keep Your Paycheck, Live Your Passion: How to Fulfil Your Dream Without Having to Quit Your Day Job.* Adams Media.

Tewe, Jimi (2011). *Free from Corporate Slavery: From Running the Rate Race to Achieving Career Success.* Inspiro Publishing.

Tewe, Olujimi O. (2004). *Where Did All My Money Go? How to Manage and Increase Your Income.* Totalbusinessman.

Tracy, Brian (2003). *Change Your Thinking Change Your Life: How to Unlock Your Potential to Success and Achievement.* John Willey and Sons Inc.

Wright, Seyi (2007). *Choose to Make a Difference: Ten Keys for Living a Complete Life.* Bluebird Communications Limited.

www.ingramcontent.com/pod-product-compliance
Lightning Source LLC
Chambersburg PA
CBHW071447070526
44578CB00001B/246